MALAMUTE MAN

Memoirs of an Arctic Traveler

Joe G. Henderson

Library of Congress Cataloging-in-Publication Data

Henderson, Joe G.
    Malamute Man: Memoirs of an Arctic Traveler

ISBN:
ISBN-13: 978-0615587660
ISBN: 0615587666

In memory of my father, Jack Henderson,
who always encouraged me to write
a book about my adventures.

Acknowledgments

I am indebted to my friend and Arctic expedition guest, Angus Mill, for allowing me to use many of the amazing photos he has taken on his trips with me and the dogs. My Arctic expeditions require a lot of assistance to launch every season and it takes a team to make it happen. I am very thankful for the generosity of Merrill Powers and family, who have braved the Dalton Highway in the dead of winter many times to deliver expedition supplies to the starting point and for getting me and the dogs back home at the end of each season. I am also incredibly grateful for our dog/house sitter, Joey Jurco, who has taken excellent care of our malamutes and our house dog, Melvin, whenever we travel.

I would like to thank Roger Burggraf, my dear friend and fellow Alaskan malamute breeder, who has always been an inspiration to me.

I have to thank Melvin, our black lab, who has so many important roles around our house—lap dog, puppy herder, guardian of the dog yard, and friend to all.

Of course, I thank every malamute I've been blessed to share my adventures with. I appreciate their loyalty.

I am grateful for the support of my loving wife, Andrea, and our beautiful baby daughter, Elaina. Andrea has stood by me in unwavering support of my Arctic expeditions, and can be credited with a lot of the behind-the-scenes work they require.

Most of all I thank the good Lord for blessing me with the opportunity to live my dream.

I would like to extend my sincere thanks to the following individuals who contributed to the funding of this book through kickstarter.com:

Josh Amos	Cheryl Henderson
Tanya Biami	Louise Jones
Kathryn Bork	Dolores van der Kolk
Chris & Pat Catsimanes	Martha Kriske
Wayne & Bryony Clark	Sylvie Lewis
Sue Crawford	Phillip Gary Smith
Marianne Downey	David Stefanoff
Bill Ford	Scott Trepanier
Pierre & Sabryna Gendron	Dennis Waite

Special thanks to the following people and organizations for their generous contributions:

Alaskan Malamute Working Association (UK)	Kent & Kathy Loveland
	Jason & Adrienne Loveland
Ryan Alford	Angus Mill
Rodney & Angela Biggs	Pulldogs.com
Mike Cossey	Kate Salvadore
Allan & Paige Delaney	Carolyn Schlick
Peter Flaig	Subzero Saints/Interior Freight Dog Association
Tim Van Gelderen	
Hilda Henderson	Bob Sutherland
Hundekjøring w/Monica Celius	Rosemary E. Wise
Louise Jones	In Memory of Gus & Helen Jivelekas
Tecla Kuhl	
Linda Lines	In Memory of Clair & Angeline Loveland

Do not go where the path may lead,
go instead where there is no path and leave a trail.
—*Ralph Waldo Emerson*

CHAPTER 1

The Makings of an Arctic Explorer

When I broke camp and hitched up the team I had a gut feeling that something was wrong, like I was leaving something behind. I glanced over my shoulder to make sure the campsite was clean and stepped on the sled runners. I hardly got out the first syllable for the command to go, and the 22 malamutes lunged ahead, nearly throwing me off the runners. They were anxious to get home. I didn't blame them. We had been on a dog sledding expedition in the Arctic for three months and I was getting antsy to get home, too, and see my wife.

As the April sun beat down on us, the dogs lost their enthusiasm and slowed to a trot. Mitch, one of the lead dogs, stumbled in a soft hole and got tangled in the lines. I stopped the team, worked my way up to assist Mitch and untangled the rope around his leg.

In the distance, from behind my sled, I heard a growl. It was a deep guttural sound that made the hairs on the back of my neck stand up. I knew what it meant and I was unarmed except for a rifle in my sled. I jumped to my feet and sprinted toward my rifle.

The grizzly was making ground fast, running straight toward me. He and I had about the same distance to go to reach my sled. My mind raced as I ran in what felt like slow motion. I

My 22 Alaskan malamute freighting team and I hauling supplies on an expedition near the Arctic coast. (photo by Yolanda Malavear)

knew we would both meet together at the sled. While running I pulled my hunting knife out and prepared to cut the ropes off the sled to access my rifle, but the bear was gaining on me. Images of the dogs and I suffering a violent death flashed in my mind, sending an extra shot of adrenaline through my veins. The bear stumbled in the soft snow, but quickly regained his composure and continued charging. I finally made it to the sled and in one swift motion, slashed the ropes and pulled out my rifle just in time to plant a bullet between his dark, determined eyes, just short of the sled.

For nearly three decades I have been fending off bears, frostbite, and brutal blizzards with my dog team in the Arctic. My malamutes are a part of me. They are as much my family as they are my friends. More than once I have put my life on the line for them and several times they have done the same for me.

***

Growing up, I always had dogs. I still remember getting my first dog, a black and white beagle who I named Prince, when I was five years old. When I got a little older, he and I became hunting partners. As the early autumn frosts layered the Michigan countryside, Prince and I would work the thickets and forests alongside the railroad tracks for cottontails every day after school. I'll never forget the sounds of my shotgun firing and the aroma of gunpowder hanging low in the hallows along the tracks. Prince's dark, trustful eyes gleamed and his tail proudly swished back and forth as he pranced back to me with a rabbit between his jaws.

There was hardly a day after school when Prince and I didn't hunt together. The weather didn't make a difference and it seemed the rainier, snowier and nastier the weather got, the better luck we had hunting. Prince was quite a hunter and that wily little beagle taught me a lot about working with dogs.

One of the lessons I learned from Prince was to just keep quiet and let him work and do what he was born to do. I remember the crackling brush and the sound of Prince panting as he zigzagged in front of me, searching for the scent of a cottontail. It was just him and I, no words or commands were necessary. Prince knew the nature of rabbits better than I did. He knew how they'd hold still until the very last moment, practically dropping drool on their ears, until they darted. He knew how to turn those quick cottontails around in a circle, allowing me to plant some lead shot in them. But most of all, Prince knew that by doing what came naturally to him, he was pleasing me. And I also knew what he loved, and that was to just hunt.

Every day after school, just like clockwork, my little shotgun's muzzle would be smoking and mom would fry up the rabbits for dinner using her special, secret recipe. Prince and I were living like kings. That kind of freedom for a kid my

3

age was the best.

As the autumn frost became covered in snow Prince and I continued to hunt the quick and elusive cottontails. Usually around Christmas the west winds pushed deep snow like waves covering the cut corn fields and thickets, making it too tough for Prince to plug through the deep snow, so I'd slip outside the house without him and go after the rabbits. I loved those wintery days with a passion. I remember the wind stinging my cheeks and how trudging through the deep powder wore me thin, and thinking that someday I'd live in place where the snow, wind and ice ruled day and night. I remember gulping the cold air as if I was trying to quench an unquenchable thirst. I just had the gut feeling that this was the training ground for my future.

As the years passed, I noticed I was getting awfully skinny and everything that I was eating went right through me, everything except meat, that is, and little did I know at the time I was stricken with gluten intolerance.

To satisfy my growing body's needs, I hunted all the more in true earnest. Meat and potatoes were on my platter every night and if the freezer ran shy of rabbits, I'd set snares and traps for those little guys, so I always had a full plate of crispy, fried meat.

Of course the Michigan countryside and forests weren't only home to rabbits but also to all kinds of other small game, like pheasants, quail, squirrels and raccoon, to name a few. And of course that just meant I had to get more hunting dogs. After all, Prince couldn't hunt everything and he definitely wasn't a match to a snarling, corn-fed coon.

Then one day, Prince didn't come back from a hunt. Just like that he was gone. The family searched hard and long for my little buddy, but to no avail. He may have disappeared that day but he stays alive in my memory chasing cottontails and prancing in pride with those trusting dark eyes looking into mine to this day.

As time passed, and to make up for the loss of Prince, I acquired several more hunting dogs including a few black and tan hounds and retrievers. Although my folks probably didn't care much for all the dogs around, I managed to keep them fed by working odd jobs and selling the coon skins that the hounds and I had harvested.

When I graduated from high school in 1979, teen restlessness caused me to throw a suitcase in my 1970 Buick Century, say my goodbyes to the family and my dogs, and start driving—to where exactly I wasn't quite sure.

I ended up in the Florida Keys. It was a far cry from Michigan farm country, brier thickets, hunting dogs and cottontails, but it was wonderful country nonetheless with miniature deer bouncing in the forests and plenty of fresh fish and spiny lobster to harvest in the Atlantic.

Sparsely populated with people, the islands had construction work readily available for anyone who wanted to work, and I mean anyone! I worked on a steel crew with characters that I thought had only existed in the movies. These guys were escaped convicts, self proclaimed warlocks, shysters and con artists. I always had to sleep with one eye open and a knife under my pillow, which by the way was nothing more than a brown burlap bag full of extra clothes. I never put much emphasis on luxury and pillows and beds were none of my concern, especially since I slept on the beach. Why not sleep on the beach, I figured. The cool evening breeze kept the mosquitoes at bay. The red sun melting into the ocean every evening was like nothing I had ever seen before. And the smell of lobster sizzling over the camp fire with stars winking at me was like living in a dream. All I needed was a beagle lying at my side.

After work every day I went scuba diving on the coral reefs, harvesting lobsters and mammoth sized grouper, not only for my food but also to sell to tourists as a source of added income. Eventually I saved enough cash to purchase a skiff with a motor and headed out to sea where I knew my real fortune was just waiting inside a sunken shipwreck.

I never did find any treasure in the form of gold coins but I did find a treasure chest of adventure. Sharks, moray eels, giant sting rays and menacing barracudas were daily encounters on the reefs I had explored and the same shooting skills I obtained in the Michigan briar patches I brought with me underwater in the form of a spear gun. Although, most of my time was spent searching for those sweet tasting lobsters, I used the spear gun often on giant groupers, or to fend off barracudas that had found my chrome regulator mouth piece enticing.

Sometimes, I'd wait until night settled on the ocean before I plunged in the depths of the reefs. Following my compass's needle and watching the time I'd motor through the blackness until I estimated my skiff was on the edge of the reef, beside the gulf streams current where the big lobster lay hiding. I had found those lobsters loved to wander amongst the jagged coral at night leaving themselves vulnerable to a quick set of hands. Spotting them with a bright underwater flashlight I'd grabbed the lobsters and stuff them into a large netted bag that I had fastened to my weight belt. As the night progressed, the bag got heavier and heavier and the reef became quite a lively scene with weird shaped, colorful fishes, crabs, sea urchins and moray eels. As I swam, hovering just above the sandy ocean floor and colorful corals, the lobsters made a strange grinding noise in the bag that sounded like rubbing a finger across a balloon. Several times, this grinding sound had alerted the entire undersea world and before long I'd have a large school of creatures attaching themselves to me and the lobster bag, including giant grouper that tugged me backwards, apparently thinking that they'd just caught their luckiest catch of the night—a bag of lobsters.

Several months quickly flew by and I became bored with

The windblown Arctic expanse.

construction work, so I tried my hand as a sailboat mate. But the wide open Atlantic, cool breeze against my face, the silver moonlight glancing off the wandering waves with the boat drifting in silence brought back memories of Prince and the hounds. It was all I could take – I had to go north, as far north as I could travel, to the Arctic. I had to quench that unquenchable thirst for invigorating cold, wide open spaces and freedom to roam and explore—alone.

***

Two years later I found myself in Alaska working for a hunting guide. After the fall hunting season I had a choice to either find a job in one of Alaska's big cities or spend winter in the mountains and run a trapline. That wasn't a hard decision to make, but first I had to find a companion to bring along. I searched the local paper and found a husky/malamute mix puppy for $50.

When the polite, white-haired lady handed me the leash with the pup, I was completely surprised. I hadn't expected such a big brute for a three month old puppy. He was a fat, black ball of fur with dark beady eyes and a creamy white patch on his chest. He looked nothing like the pups I had grown up with. My dogs had always been scrawny, wiry, and hyper with eyes that darted in search of a rabbit or raccoon to chase.

I named him Takhin, which means *snow* in the Tlingit Indian language. I set him in the cab of my old 1964 pickup truck and headed down the road to the small town of Haines.

It was a brisk morning and the town was just waking up. The sidewalks were desolate, but the sporting goods store was open, so I purchased four boxes of ammunition, traps, and a pair of snowshoes, then drove up the highway to a winding dirt road which led us to the edge of the Chilkat River.

Dust was blowing off a sandbar and geese were flying overhead in large flocks. Across the river, beyond the tall spruce trees bowing over the bank, was a shaded forest and jagged, snow-covered mountain peaks. The land looked raw and brutally rugged. That's where Takhin and I were going. I had planned to find an old log cabin that a friend had given me a map with directions to, and live there for the winter trapping pine marten. First though, I had to secure a supply of meat for the winter.

I pulled the canoe out of the truck bed, set it in the water and loaded my gear and meager supply of groceries into it. The only food I packed to live off was 90 lbs of dried salmon, moose meat, salt, and lard. I figured Takhin and I would live off the land. I was used to a meat diet and I was sure he wouldn't object to eating meat for the entire six months of winter either. My other gear consisted of a rifle, tent, axe, winter clothing, a small toboggan, and more traps.

I sat Takhin in the canoe and pushed off. The paddle went deep into the river's powerful current as the canoe cut through the white caps. Takhin's eyes widened when the waves slapped the bow and spray splashed over the sides.

I worked the paddle until we reached the opposite shore of the Chilkat where the tall forest stood looming over us. After a short search along the shore, I found the tributary that led us to our new log cabin home.

It was almost dark when I arrived at the cabin that was hidden in the Sitka spruce away from the river's edge. I stepped over a pile of fresh bear crap as I approached the door, opened the chamber of my rifle and dropped a cartridge in. My heart banged on my chest like a hammer when the sounds of pots and pans rattled from inside the dark cabin. Sweat beaded on my forehead, and my hands started to shake. I heard the bear's low grunt. I had never encountered a bear face to face before. I'd heard and read stories of bears attacking people, and eating them alive. The images were playing in my mind like a horror movie as I cautiously pushed open the creaky hinged door with the toe of my rubber boot. My trigger finger was itching to start blasting into the darkness, but I held my composure and held my rifle steady for the imminent charge, hoping to fire off a round that would do him in. Then I heard a growl and brush breaking outside the window. I held my breath and listened. Silence filled the room. I took a deep breath. As my eyes adjusted to the darkness, I realized that the bear had been there, and had used the window as an entry and an exit.

I offloaded the supplies and gear from the canoe, and set a burlap sack of dried salmon beside the door along with my sleeping bag. Inside, it reeked of bear crap. I tossed the bear crap out the door, picked up the pots and pans, chopped some wood and fired up the rusty wood stove. After covering the broken window with a canvas tarp, I lit the two candles lying on the old wooden table and had the cabin feeling like home in no time.

Snow started to fall as I blew the candles out and settled into my sleeping bag for the night. Takhin curled up next to my feet on an old wool blanket. He was exhausted.

Awakened early in the morning by teeth and claws tearing into the burlap sack of dried salmon, I sprang out of my sleeping bag, Takhin yipped as I stumbled over him, I grabbed my rifle and swung open the door. The bear took off running with the bag of salmon clinched in his teeth and disappeared in the woods. Takhin went after him, but stopped short to eat a piece of dried salmon that had fallen out of the sack.

"Son of a bitch!" I yelled. Takhin dropped the fish, cocked his head sideways and looked at me. I don't think he had ever heard me speak yet, let alone cuss. I had no one to blame but myself for losing the fish. I shouldn't have left it outside. That salmon was like gold to us.

After salvaging a few salmon strips that had fallen out of the bag, Takhin and I spent the rest of the day exploring the surrounding forest. He was as curious as I was. I had never seen such large trees before. The trunks of the Sitka spruce were six feet in diameter, and creaked and moaned in the wind. It seemed that it was always dark in the forest, especially on a cloudy day, but it looked like good marten habitat.

Pine marten were the bread and butter in the fur trade at that time. They are similar to mink, only larger with thick, sable fur. I caught my first pine marten in northern British Columbia a year earlier. With the assistance of local Indians, I had acquired many of the trapping and hunting skills that helped me transition into that lifestyle in Alaska.

I calculated that if I caught enough pine marten to sell at the auction in the spring, I'd be able to purchase more dogs, put together a large team, and move to the Arctic. I had always been intrigued with the far north my entire life and wanted more than ever to go there.

Standing in front of one of my old trapping cabins.

The temperature dropped quickly that evening as I sorted through my meager rations. The bear had taken a lot of my dried salmon and I figured I'd better get an early start in the morning to hunt for moose.

As darkness fell on the forest, I piled the food on the cabin roof in case the bear came back. Then I melted some lard and lubed the door hinges with it so it opened and closed quietly. Both Takhin and I ate a moose steak and settled down on my sleeping bag with the rifle beside me. I figured the bear would be back.

Late that night, I heard a twig break and my heart jumped. Takhin stood up with his long black hackles raised and growled. "Quiet, you little mutt, and stay right there," I whispered to the frightened pup. Slowly, I felt my way across the cabin with my rifle, and eased the door open. The bear caught sight of me and ran into the trees.

One of the creeks running through my trapline.

I stepped outside, and with the glow of the moon shining down through the trees, I saw the bear standing up on his two hind legs, facing me, about a stone's throw away. There was a lot of brush between us, so I stepped to my right, away from the brush, where I could get a clean shot at him.

As soon as he saw me move, the bear charged. I pulled the rifle up to my shoulder, squeezed the trigger and planted a bullet into his chest. That really ticked him off. He slid to a stop and let out a strange cry, regained his composure, and charged again so fast that I didn't have time to chamber another round.

I stepped backwards into the thick alder brush and the bear dove for my legs, but missed and grabbed an alder tree between his teeth instead. The tree splintered as he swung his massive head from side to side, giving me enough time to shoot, shattering his shoulder. I thought the bear was mad before, holy smokes, he was ripping apart every tree in his path and my legs were scrambling backwards as fast as I could move them, all the while chambering another round and shooting him again. His left shoulder dragged on the ground now, but he kept coming with vengeance. When I felt my back against a big spruce tree, Takhin started barking and yapping behind the bear. I watched the bear's dark eyes turn toward him, which gave me the opportunity to squeeze off the final round at point blank range, killing him. When I caught my breath and I started to come down from my adrenaline rush, I praised Takhin and assured him that he wasn't a little mutt after all.

The bear weighed at least 600 lbs and was fat as a hog. I figured he had been eating blueberries in the mountains, storing up fat for the winter. I cut the meat in strips, dried it in the smoke house, and rendered the lard, which amounted to about three gallons. Takhin drooled over the smoked meat and devoured a large portion of it. I have to admit, it wasn't bad tasting meat. I was glad to have a nice reserve of meat, but could've done without getting it the way I did.

My old wall tent at a trapping camp.

A few days later I hiked up the river valley in search of pine marten. Their tracks were scarce and I realized that in order to make my trapping venture profitable, I had to leave the cabin for a richer pine martin habitat. I loaded the canoe with my supplies and started pulling it upriver. Takhin had the time of his life running alongside me in the trees, chasing little red squirrels that chattered at him in defiance.

The river narrowed and wound through the trees, eventually becoming too shallow for the canoe. It was much colder in the higher elevations, and deep snow covered the mountain sides and the forest floor. I found a clear, level area beside the river, pushed the snow aside with my snowshoes and set up my canvas wall tent. There were lots of marten prints under the trees and some wolverine tracks as well. The trees were much smaller in diameter compared to the trees by the cabin and I could see a glacier further up the river by some high cliffs with goats feeding on grasses protruding out of the snow.

After cooking a quick cup of coffee on the tent's woodstove

I ventured off with Takhin to try to add some goat meat to our menu. We were back in camp within an hour with a nice fat billy goat.

Not long after that, I found out that wolves were partial to goat meat as well. While Takhin and I were outside our tent, I watched one of the wolves, a large black one, stalk a billy goat. He slowly worked his way above the goat while two other wolves kept the goat's attention by playing with each other, below on the cliff. Once positioned, the wolf leaped, and body slammed the goat, sending both goat and wolf rolling down the snowy slope to the cliff where the other wolves were waiting. That night while the three wolves feasted on the goat, they howled up a storm. I couldn't sleep at all. I'd get out of the sleeping bag, light a candle and then the wolves would stop, but as soon as I blew the candle out, they'd howl like crazy again. This went on repeatedly until finally I was fit to be tied. I stormed out of the tent and hollered at the wolves, calling them every name in the book. They never howled again for the rest of the night.

Eventually, the wolves grew comfortable around Takhin and me. Sometimes they would slither and sneak behind us on the trail. They were especially interested in Takhin, and I am sure he looked like an easy meal to them.

The wolves were vicious amongst themselves. Early one morning while we were camped next to a warm, ice-free pond that was loaded with fish, Takhin and I woke up to the loudest raucous of snarling, growling, and whimpering I'd ever heard. Two wolves, apparently fighting over a large fish, were in a death grip with one another. Takhin started to bolt toward them, but I grabbed his collar and held him so he wouldn't get in the middle of their brawl. The wolves fought for a few minutes then limped away, and all was silent again. Investigating the scene at daylight, the blood-stained snow was packed down with wolf tracks, claw marks and patches of black fur, but there were no casualties.

I didn't mind the wolves around. They were both entertaining and interesting, but because my main focus was catching pine marten, which was a full time job. I never bothered the wolves as long as they didn't come after Takhin.

As the snow kept piling up deeper through November and into December, Takhin grew taller, broader shouldered and tough as nails. It was time to harness my buddy so he could lend a hand in pulling the toboggan. I made him a perfectly tailored harness out of moose hide. Now, with him harnessed to the toboggan and me pulling with a rope, we covered more territory and caught more pine marten. We were a team, whether it was pulling, packing supplies, or just relaxing around the campfire. We were always together and had a strong bond between us.

Takhin and I continued venturing farther into the forest, exploring, trapping and hunting. Sometimes, the forest would be too dense and thick with brush for us to pull the toboggan. So I sewed a saddle pack out of canvas for Takhin to carry supplies in while I shouldered a back pack. Between the two of us, we carried all of our supplies, even the pine marten as we caught them. I had temporarily abandoned the canvas tent because of its heavy weight and bulkiness.

Camping under the open sky wasn't bad at all. I enjoyed watching the campfire sparks rise toward the bright stars, the aroma of steaks sizzling over the hot coals and capturing the warmth on a cold night. I loved the freedom to roam and camp where I wanted in the raw, unrefined wilderness. Sitting beside the campfire every night, I skinned and stretched the pine marten I had caught that day, and afterwards Takhin and I feasted on wild game meat. We also had Labrador leaves for tea and rosehips, which I had gathered earlier in the winter. They were a great source of vitamin C, which kept scurvy at bay.

The down side of living on the trail in southeast Alaska

was the weather. It was sporadic. It would rain one day and snow the next. Hypothermia was a real threat when my clothes became soaked and heavy. It didn't bother Takhin. He was always high-spirited and rearing to go an extra mile. Although I always had the opportunity to dry my clothes and warm my feet beside a blazing hot campfire every night, I often welcomed days when the temperature plummeted below zero. At least when it was cold I could stay dry.

I remember the night I had experienced the coldest temperatures that winter. It was around Christmas and the temperature dropped to –36°F. I had built my usual campfire by shoveling snow off an area beside a giant Sitka spruce, laying long, dry logs parallel to one another on the ground and stacking them on top of each other, and then setting the whole pile of wood ablaze. Sitting beside the fire was comfortable, but I knew my sleeping bag wasn't adequate for those temperatures, and I had to find a way to stay warm. After I had roasted a steak over the coals for dinner and tossed Takhin some meat, I put the fire out and carefully scraped all the hot coals aside. The ground was very warm where the fire had been, perfect for a bed. I laid my canvas tarp over the hot ground, rolled out my sleeping bag, crawled in and slept comfortably with Takhin curled up on his moose hide mat at my feet. From then on, I repeated the campfire hot bed every night.

As the months passed, Takhin and I ventured further up the river, traversing across the glaciers and climbing the mountains. It became difficult to focus on trapping anymore when there was so much country to explore. Takhin grew bigger by the day, and I became lean and proficient at subsisting off the land. I didn't want it to end. I wanted to stay in the wilderness and explore further into the mountains, and farther north, but I knew sooner or later I would have to return to civilization.

Then one night, as the moon crested the jagged mountain peaks and wolves howled in the distance I whispered a prayer.

It was a prayer the Lord granted me. I asked God to guide me further north to the Arctic where I could explore and travel in its vast, untouched wilderness with Takhin and a team of malamutes.

As the snow started to melt, and flocks of geese flew overhead, I loaded the canoe with all my worldly possessions, including a large bundle of pine marten skins, and pushed off. Takhin and I drifted down the winding tributary, shot through rapids, almost got tipped over by a sweeper, and then drifted out on the muddy Chilkat River. I worked the canoe across the river to my truck. Takhin jumped out of the heavily loaded canoe behind me, hackles up and growling like a charging bear.

"C'mon Takhin, it's just a darn truck," I reassured him. He cocked his head, and then peed on the tire.

That spring, the marten skins sold for top dollar at the Canadian raw fur auction, and the following winter we headed north to the Arctic.

CHAPTER 2

North to the Arctic

After working hard at a logging camp that summer on a remote southeast Alaska island, I loaded my old pickup with Takhin and all my worldly possessions and drove as far north as my old pickup would take us.

When my truck limped into Coldfoot with a nearly empty tank of gas, covered in mud, and the last spare tire going flat, I discovered Coldfoot wasn't the thriving little town I had thought. It consisted of a small truck stop and fuel station, tire shop, restaurant and post office, but it was strategically located half way between Fairbanks and Prudhoe Bay on the infamous Haul road, or "kamikaze trail" as the truck drivers called it, which was 550 miles of mud and gravel. And muddy it was. Apparently, there had been a record amount of rainfall which saturated the road and transformed it into a mud bog. The road looked as mucked up as a cattle trail through a swamp. The mud stuck to the truck and tires like snot and dripped and oozed off the fenders.

Luckily, I had a set of tire chains for driving through the worst parts of the road. But the mud became the least of my worries when the truck finally got up to a decent speed and we came upon a stretch of steep hills and sharp switchback turns. I felt more at ease with a grizzly bear charging me than driving on that road. I have to admit, credit has to be given to those truckers who drove the Haul road back then when that road was so rough. They were the most courageous, generous, and helpful men and women I had ever met. I don't know how many times they had offered to help me as I nursed the truck to Coldfoot.

Coldfoot was established during the gold rush around 1900. Back then it was the hub for local miners, merchants, prospectors, and prostitutes. But after a few years there was a new gold strike 16 miles up the Koyukuk River and the new village of Wiseman, named after the gentleman who discovered gold there, was built. As Wiseman grew, Coldfoot succumbed to the slow death of abandonment and decay. After the completion of the Trans-Alaska pipeline in 1977, however, the town of Coldfoot was resurrected.

Coldfoot and Wiseman are situated in the Brooks Range foothills and in the midst of rolling hills and mountains, layered with black spruce trees, large meadows of sweet blueberries, and crystalline streams that are loaded with arctic grayling. There were plenty of moose, caribou, dall sheep, bears, wolves, and pine marten around, too—everything a trapper would want. There were several small villages and gold mining communities north of Coldfoot as well. Wiseman was the largest community and had a population of about 20 folks from all walks of life—commercial fisherman, dog mushers, hunting guides, gold miners, drifters, and hippies. It was accessible from the Dalton Highway, about three miles down a twisted dirt road which was hardly compatible for a vehicle, but it was a road nonetheless.

What caught my eye first when I drove into Wiseman were two large, handsome, black and white Alaskan malamutes lying outside the door of an old log cabin. Smoke spiraled out of the chimney and the curtain pulled back as my pickup passed. The yard was littered with rusty wheel barrels, shovels, oil drums, a bull dozer and other equipment that you'd expect to find at a gold mine. It was noon, and the village seemed eerily quiet as I drove past a log cabin with boarded up doors and windows and willow brush sprouting out of the roof. The narrow road led me across a shallow creek and rounded a sharp bend where I noticed a small cabin tucked in the trees. There was a flourishing vegetable garden in the yard and a stack of split firewood by the door. It looked like a peaceful residence. Then I passed by a large, glaring white satellite dish beside a sagging cabin with two small airplanes in the yard, a deafening generator by the wood shed, and a growling Saint Bernard/husky mix tethered to a tree.

After spending a few weeks getting acquainted with folks in Wiseman, I had the opportunity to visit with a couple old timers there. Their stories of Wiseman's frontier history intrigued me. I remember one gentleman I visited had a remarkable memory and talent for telling stories about Wiseman when it was a thriving metropolis of over 100 people. His place was warm and comfortable and coffee brewed slowly on the crackling wood burning stove while he brought the good old days to life. He related his experiences with such passion and detail I envisioned clearly what life was like in the early 1900's. I could hear the tavern's phonograph playing through the long summer nights while the midnight sun flared over the mountain peaks. I could visualize gold miners celebrating with dancing girls, swinging, and laughing in the dusty streets, drunkards staggering, sled dogs fighting, a murderer captured and chained in a makeshift jail, prospectors selling their worldly possessions paying off a gambling debt, sobering men and women walking to church at dawn wearing their Sunday's best. But Wiseman wasn't the only town around. The most notorious town was Nolan Creek.

Nolan Creek was a few miles further down the road. The town was surrounded by rolling hills and a small, muddy stream flowing down the middle of the valley with weathered

A pile of gold after a day of sluicing.

log cabins built along the creek, some of which were inhabited and some abandoned and allowed to bow and crumble from the arctic elements.

Nolan had the nostalgia of an old western ghost town—

abandoned, forgotten, left to the elements to decay what was once a thriving town of the early 1900's. But lurking underneath the cabins and deep underground were tons of gold. The miners that worked Nolan Creek were silent about their finds of heavy, thumb-sized nuggets. They were like all the typical miners at that time. They drove old beat up pickup trucks, wore tattered clothing, and talked as if they were always broke. But Nolan Creek was one of the richest gold mines in Alaska. There were about a dozen callous-handed miners there, quietly working their claims. They were a friendly crew, although a little protective of their mining claims. An occasional bullet flying over the head of a trespasser wasn't uncommon but as long as you stayed away from their claims they were friendly. I don't blame the miners for trying to scare folks out of the area. They worked hard for their gold and it seemed like every con artist, thief, claim jumper, and federal government regulator was trying to steal their claims. If those miners didn't know you, they didn't trust you. For that matter, they didn't trust each other either, because there were quite a few shoot-outs amongst them, most of which resulted in harmless window shattering, although there were some dead serious gun fights on occasion. But the miners who kept their cool and learned to relish in hard work and the free lifestyle that goes along with mining and finding enough gold to make a good living, well, those folks lived a life that most men only dream about.

Despite the rough-around-the-edges atmosphere of Nolan Creek, I got to know a few good folks there and decided to settle there for the winter. I felt most of the miners and I had plenty in common. We cherished freedom, hard work, and living off the land. So, before the onslaught of winter, I moved into an old log cabin on Nolan Creek and went to work building a dog sled out of birch wood. It was a fine and sturdy sled, except I needed material to protect the bottom of the runners so they wouldn't splinter and wear out.

I searched around at the Nolan Creek junk yard, which seemed at first glance to be nothing more than a pile of abandoned vehicles, and met a grizzled old gold miner. He was thin as a rail and had a holstered revolver, the barrel of which hung to his knee. His beard was peppered white and his mustache stained yellow from tobacco smoke. He asked me what the hell I was looking for. His dark, leathery face and blue eyes brightened as I quickly explained my dog sled runner dilemma. He said he had exactly what I wanted and led me behind his dilapidated cabin where he pulled two long, rusty strips of steel from the willow brush. He claimed he had used it on the bottom of his sled runners when he worked as a freighter a few years prior. He was a cheerful old-timer, enthusiastic and curious about my dog mushing endeavors. I asked him if he had some adventure stories he could tell me about from his dog mushing days.

"Nope, adventures are for green horns!" he spouted out, along with his chew.

Eventually he loosened up and mentioned he freighted supplies to his mine with his malamutes and wished he still had them. I caught a glimpse of a tear when he said they were his family.

Over time, I acquired some dogs from the local folks at Nolan and Wiseman. One of the most memorable sled dogs I got was Bruiser, and I remember distinctly the day I met him.

"This is Bruiser. He's a man-eater and a mean s.o.b and if he chews your arm off, don't tell me I didn't warn you," John said as we walked toward the large reddish-white Alaskan malamute chained to a dwarfed spruce tree.

When John (we'll call him that for the sake of anonymity), a dog musher friend and a neighbor of mine at the time, said he had a dog for me, I didn't expect it would be a "man-eating s.o.b."

As I chuckled, assuming John was joking, I reached out to

pet Bruiser.

"Hold it! Don't move too fast," John said, grabbing my shirt sleeve. "He'll take your damn hand off."

John told me he got Bruiser in the early spring from an old gold miner that had passed on. He ran Bruiser with his team of huskies, but Bruiser scared the crap out of him with his constant growling, so for some reason John decided that Bruiser was out to get him.

In reality, Bruiser was just a typical Alaskan malamute, a very misunderstood creature with an ancient genealogy that is traced back thousands of years. No doubt Bruiser was a rough looking character with a scar running across his muzzle, piercing brown eyes, paws that would rival those of a grizzly bear, and a solid frame that shouldered 150 lbs of solid muscle.

Bruiser's hackles stood up as John reached and fastened a leash on his collar and handed it to me. Bruiser's tail drooped low as I led him down the narrow dirt road. As we approached the cabin, my four dogs saw us and howled mournfully like I had found their long lost brother.

Bruiser's tail curled tightly over his back. He recognized the sounds of his own kind, his brothers and cousins. He longed for companionship with someone like himself, other dogs to play and wrestle with. He'd had enough of being chained to that tree in the woods far away from John's other dogs with no companions except menacing mosquitoes and an occasional red squirrel chattering and scolding him. He was lonely and that made him mean. I placed my hand between his ears, and lightly stroked his thick fur while we walked. Bruiser tossed his head up, our eyes met, and then he lunged ahead nearly jerking my arm off. I ran behind him holding onto the leash while he pulled me toward the dog yard.

My other dogs whined as I tethered him on a long chain beside Bandit, a burgundy colored, yearling malamute. Bruiser's hackles raised and his legs stiffened as he swung his hip around in Bandit's face. Bandit stretched out and sniffed his butt. Bruiser growled like a bear. Then he turned, lowered his massive paw on Bandits shoulder, and pushed him to the dirt. Bandit got up and charged. The two malamutes collided and dust rose around them as they played, wrestled and chewed on each other until their fur was drenched in drool. Panting heavily in the hot sun, they lay beside each other, exhausted, and slept for a while. When they woke, they wrestled again until the midnight sun shaved the mountain peaks.

As the rivers froze that winter and knee deep snow covered the tundra I went to work sewing together five new moose hide single-tree harnesses for the team, but on Bruiser's harness I added a special touch. I sewed an extra layer of winter caribou hide onto the chest piece, making it really soft for my big baby. I have found that the larger an Alaskan malamute is, the more babyish they are. So when it comes to getting these big fellas to work, I knew I had to gain their trust and love by going the extra mile. That being said, malamutes are amazingly tough-minded brutes and can endure the Arctic's brutal environment with a wagging tail and a smile.

After finishing the harnesses and sled, I hitched up the dogs. My other dogs were a bunch of malamute mixes. Takhin was a medium sized black malamute/husky mix, and young like Bandit. Blue was a large and handsome gray malamute that was built like Bruiser, and Mitch was my leader. He was a 100 lb black and white, very intelligent malamute.

Bruiser hated Mitch's guts. I knew he hated Mitch from the start. When I hitched Bruiser in wheel position he pierced Mitch with a deadly glare and growled, like he wanted to tear him to pieces. Some dogs just have a dominant aura about them that other dogs can sense, and Mitch was one of those dogs. Mitch thought he was tough and intimidated Bruiser with his strutting and hackle-raising, arrogant behavior. Mitch was a good command leader though, and I really loved him and

Breaking trail.

wished the two rivals would get along. I knew they would get along eventually. It seems most dogs that share hard work will form a bond with one another, kind of like soldiers when they experience battle together.

As soon as I harnessed Bruiser, he jumped up and harness banged like a giant maniacal fool. The other dogs turned their heads and watched his ridiculous, energy wasting behavior as they listened for my command to go. There's nothing worse than harness banging malamutes. They are so powerful that they can pull the snow hook and head down the trail without you. But most dogs learn by watching their peers and it didn't take long for Bruiser to figure it out. Eventually Bruiser settled down and learned to sit like the others while hitching up.

That first winter, those five dogs and I traveled hundreds of miles together. Most of the time the sled was heavily loaded so I never had the opportunity to stand on the runners of my new freight sled. I spent most of my time on snowshoes busting trail in front of Mitch or holding the gee pole and steering the heavy sled.

They were a fine team though, well-behaved and tougher than heck. We broke trail, pitched camp, and explored the mountains. It was a time of freedom. The stars were my ceiling and boreal forest was my home. My bed was a caribou hide spread out on the snow and a crackling campfire with the malamutes' howl was my music. Every night while the aroma of sweet wood smoke filled the air I watched the Northern Lights on the sky's stage. Sometimes they flowed like ocean waves overhead in an array of colors and other times they danced and swirled in hazy green. And one night they shot overhead as red as blood.

When the mercury sunk to -60°F it didn't bother the dogs at all. I adapted to the cold and was quite comfortable in my homemade caribou fur mukluks, mitts, and heavy parka.

I noticed during blizzards though, while Bandit hunkered down, Bruiser seemed to lay in comfort. Bruiser's coat was thick and impenetrable to the cold, but Bandit's fur was long and wooly and it collected snow, requiring constant combing and attention.

I also noticed Bruiser appeared to have an exceptionally low metabolism that enabled him to stay fat and healthy during the coldest times in winter. Bruiser also had a great attitude no matter how badly Mother Nature beat us up with windstorms and deep snow. His big, brushy tail was always curled and waving. It seemed that Bruiser was the perfect Alaskan malamute, except he still hated Mitch with passion.

Then one day we hit waist deep snow on the river, and Mitch couldn't get through it. He struggled at every step. Mitch was just too small. The snow just swallowed him up, even though I was busting trail for him. But it looked like Bruiser was plowing through it effortlessly with his broad chest and wide shoulders. So, I placed Bruiser in lead and hitched Mitch in wheel. Mitch was unhappy with his demotion, but Bruiser came alive. He excitedly followed right behind me, and the snow looked like it just melted away from him as he pushed through it. He was like a snow plow and nothing slowed him down.

Later on, we traveled to the headwaters of the river and started to ascend a mountain pass. The snow became punchy with a layer of hard pack on top. Bruiser's heavy paws busted through the hard pack snow at each step, and now he struggled. So I switched him with Mitch whose lighter weight enabled him to stay on top of the crusted layer. Even though fresh snow covered his neck and shoulders, he kept the team moving.

Bruiser thought that was poor idea and he let me know it. He whined like a big baby in wheel and pulled as hard as he could. I just couldn't stand to see Bruiser in such a pathetic state of mind, exhausting himself. Some dogs just love to lead and once they have gotten a taste of what life is like up front they just can't get enough—they get addicted.

I decided to take a gamble and place both Mitch and Bruiser in lead together. They growled, showed off their sharp canines and sized each other up, but before they had a chance to divulge in a brawl I gave them the command to go. They continued growling and snarling as they leaned into their harnesses, although now their aggression was spent breaking trail. From that day on those guys became enduring comrades in harness.

Later that season, with my supplies dwindling dangerously low, the team and I climbed over a mountain pass and I found myself standing on the Continental Divide viewing the Arctic's vast landscape. I was awestruck. The treeless wilderness looked desolate and brutally lonely, yet strangely inviting. The towering mountains stood torn and sharp above the rolling hills to the north. The immense white expanse struck a chord in me. It was like arriving home after a very, very long journey. And I knew that the team felt the same way. Bruiser stared off in the expanse. This was where his ancestors originated, this was his

In the Brooks Range near the Continental Divide.

homeland. Right then and there I made a vow to Bruiser that we'd come back every winter.

I knew the Arctic was where my heart was and I had to see and explore more of it. If I were to venture into the high Arctic I had to have a dog breed that could easily endure the climate. I knew my life would rely on the dogs. They had to be well-trained, stout, healthy, and the leaders would have to meet the challenges of navigating on the open and windblown tundra. The Alaskan malamute fit the criteria. Their strong survival instincts and intelligence far surpassed any other dog I had ever worked with. They had what it took to live in the Arctic.

CHAPTER 3

Icy Predicaments

The Coldfoot area infamously lived up to its reputation as one of the coldest regions in North America. I was there the day the temperatures reached a record low of -82°F at the Coldfoot truck stop. I remember it well. I was running my trapline with the team and camping along the trail. The morning sky was a deep shade of gray and clouds of ice fog hovered over the dogs as they lay curled up in the snow. My breath crackled when I exhaled, and when I pulled my parka hood back to clear the frost off my eye lashes, it felt like bees were stinging my cheeks. I didn't think much of it. I just knew it was colder than the day before. I prepared my usual fried moose meat with coffee for breakfast then fed the team. The cold seemed to invigorate the dogs and they were rearing to go. I had about one day of travel to get back home. When I gave the command to go, the dogs lunged forward in their harnesses and sprinted a short distance, slowing down to a walk. *What the heck? There is something wrong. Maybe the dogs are tired.* I leaned into the sled and pushed up and down, but the team refused to speed up. I cussed the dogs for being lazy. Well, that didn't work so I petted and encouraged them to pull harder. That didn't work either.

I remember my thigh muscles burning with fatigue from

A typical cold day in paradise.

pushing the sled, but the dogs and I never did get that sled moving any quicker. It was tough work but we managed get back to the cabin by night fall. After feeding and taking care of the dogs I glanced at the thermometer hanging outside my door. The thermometer readings only went down to -60°F but the mercury was buried far below that mark.

Later that night a neighbor came over for a visit. He said it had been -80°F earlier that day and warned me not to go outside in those cold temperatures otherwise I would freeze my lungs. I told him that I thought it felt a little chilly, and thanked him for the lung-freezing tip, but I thought that whole concept was bull crap. I would have frozen my lungs solid pushing the sled all day, but the -80°F did explain why the sled dragged so hard on the snow.

In the Arctic, the texture of the snow changes with the wind and temperature conditions so when it's excessively cold or

Two year old expedition rookie, Red.

windy the snow dries to the consistency of sand. Eventually, I thought of a strategy to minimize the drag on the runners in cold weather. Every morning before traveling, I turned the sled over and poured water on the steel runners and let it freeze into a smooth layer of ice. It helped the sled glide better, but the ice wore out every few hours. After the ice eroded and the sled started to drag again, I'd stop the team beside some dead spruce trees, chop them down and build a blazing campfire to melt snow in my coffee pot and repeat the ice-glazing routine.

While the water was freezing to the runners, I took the opportunity to brew coffee and toss the dogs a meat snack. Before long, the scheduled campfire stop became an anticipated part of my day. It didn't take long for the dogs to figure out when break-time was, too. I swear they have clocks in their heads. If I traveled past the anticipated break time they'd slow down to a snail's pace, look over their shoulders and glare at me like I was cruelly starving them. They reminded me of little

My old homemade sled with steel runners outside my trapping cabin.

kids being deprived of a cookie. That's when I started to realize that the Alaskan malamute is a very special and intelligent dog. Just like children, they are emotional creatures and they love to see what they can get away with.

Since then, my approach to training the Alaskan malamute has been mostly psychological. Sometimes I feel like a dog psychiatrist dealing with them. There has to be a strong bond between musher and his team. It's what drives the malamute. It's their catalyst to work hard for you. Their world is centered on love for the musher and pleasing him or her. Most importantly, the lead dogs must possess this trait. A good lead dog knows exactly what the musher expects and offers it with an enthusiastic disposition.

My best leaders have always been my house dogs. Inside the home is where the strongest bonds are formed. The lead dogs also have to be intelligent, athletic, and the strongest willed dog in the team. Their sharp decision making skills can make the difference between life or death for the team and musher. There have been many instances where if it weren't for my lead dog's quick, instinctive reactions I would not have made it.

One lead dog who exhibited this quick reaction with strong survival instinct was Chief. His God given instincts were the only thing that kept us from extinction one late November day when I was hunting caribou. The weather was crisp, about -35°F, and a light blanket of snow covered the arctic tundra. It was a fine morning with all the malamutes' tails in the air as we trekked across the open landscape. Chief's black and white coat glistened in the golden sunrise, his tail curled especially tight and bristled over his back with pride. At two years of age, he was leading my team of 12 malamutes. It must be an overwhelming joy for a malamute to lead his peers. As we crested a low hill, I saw a large frozen lake in the valley with a herd of bull caribou on the far side of the lake. Their antlers rose and fell as they fed on mosses, oblivious to our approach.

Chief saw them and his enthusiasm infected the rest of the dogs. I hung on tight as the team sprinted toward them and the sled bounced across the frozen tussocks to the lake's edge. I stopped the team, grabbed my axe and walked out onto the ice. A half a dozen chops into the splintering ice assured me it was thick enough for us to safely cross. I tossed the axe into the sled, stepped on the runners and gave the command to go. Chief and the team jumped ahead on the smooth lake ice and we sailed straight for the caribou.

We were crossing a lake when the sounds of ice cracked like gunfire under the sled runners.

"Get going Chief!" I yelled to the lead dog. Suddenly it felt like the whole lake dropped out beneath us. Before I knew it, the sled was teetering over broken ice slabs twice the size of picnic tables and a foot thick. A few dogs whined and quit pulling when their paws punched through the cracks of the floating ice chunks that were supporting us. I knew if we stopped for one

Thin river ice.

second, the weight of the sled would cause them to topple over and dump us all into the blood chilling water.

"Pick it up boys," I calmly commanded, knowing the dogs fed off my emotions. The last thing I wanted was the team to panic and lose their fluid momentum over the cracking lake ice.

As the sounds of ice snapping and splintering intensified, cold chills shot up my spine and my heart seemed to rise up and stick in my throat. I held my breath and wrapped my mitts tightly onto the handlebars, I knew in my gut our luck would run out soon. I could actually smell the fishy, brackish water lapping at my mukluks. Suddenly the main leader, Chief took a hard right turn.

"C'mon, buddy!" I yelled excitedly, yet at the same time worried about Chief's erratic behavior. The other leaders sensed his confidence and kicked into high gear. Chief detected better

The team crossing glare ice.

ice under his paws and he went for it! The cold air felt strangely refreshing against my cheeks as we picked up speed across the lake with the sounds of cracking ice fading behind us. With a sigh of relief and thankfulness my heart finally migrated back down to my chest when those runners hit the shore.

Before crossing the lake, I had checked the thickness of the ice. It was plenty thick to cross. What I didn't know was that the water level in the lake had dropped several feet after it had frozen. This caused a hollow space between the water and ice, similar to a bridge, only a weak bridge that collapsed instantly under us.

***

I have to admit, that wasn't my first experience with thin ice breaking underneath me. That scenario on the lake brought back not-so-enjoyable memories.

It happened while living in northern British Columbia. I had leased a trapline from an old native man. I had caught a fair amount of pine marten and foxes during November and early December, but around Christmas my catch dwindled drastically when the temperatures fell to -40°F.

Most of the pine marten went to higher elevations where temperatures remained mild. I decided to extend my trapline further up the mountains, hoping to increase my harvest. I put a dozen traps, a hatchet, a chunk of frozen moose meat for bait, and a .22 caliber revolver in my backpack and headed down the trail.

There weren't many pine marten tracks in the snow that morning, but there was a red fox trail that zigzagged through the trees. I followed his tracks to a meadow and then onto a small, frozen beaver pond. About half way across the pond he had doubled backed a few steps and scrambled into the forest. I was curious what had startled him and caused his erratic behavior.

As I was examining the tracks, I thought about something an old native friend once told me. He had said that one of the secrets in trapping was to spark the animal's curiosity and entice them to take that last step into the trap. I took a step forward and a sharp crack broke the silence. The ice gave way under my mukluks and down I went into the frigid water. It appeared I had fallen prey to the fox's trap.

As I dropped through the hole, I remember seeing the broken edge of the ice shave past my nose, and then my vision became blurry. The shocking, cold water nearly caused my heart to explode. I looked up at the opening that was slipping from me as every muscle fiber instinctively went into action, kicking and thrashing. As my mind raced and struggled to grasp what had just happened it seemed that time slowed to a crawl. I was living in the moment, thinking no further than my body's immediate labored motions.

Opening my eyes wide, I looked down at the black abyss and panic overtook me. I reached up desperately, pulling and kicking, while holding my breath with lungs that were ready to burst. As I surfaced again, I inhaled water and battered my face against the ice. I reached for something to grab onto but there was nothing to pull myself out. I hung to the edge of the ice with one hand and tried to peel the heavy backpack off with the other, but I lost my grip on the ice and went under again. I somehow pulled myself back to the surface, fighting until I became winded and weak. *I'm not giving up! I'm still alive and too young to die!*

I felt another surge of strength and tried pulling myself out. Calming my panic, I reached out as far as I could, pushed the snow away, and rested my drenched parka sleeves on the bare ice. I looked up through the spruce and birch tree branches toward the towering mountains and whispered a three word prayer. *Please, God...help.*

With a shot of adrenalin, I kicked and pulled with everything I had left. My sleeves had frozen slightly to the ice, giving me some traction to pull, but I cannot explain how I went flying out of that water so quickly. It was like someone picked me up, and threw me face down on the ice with my feet still thrashing in the water. *I can't believe it—thank you, Lord!*

I wasted no time getting off the pond and into the safety of the trees. I tossed my pack under a spruce tree and kicked the ankle deep snow off the moss. Fighting through the overwhelming pain of my rapidly freezing extremities, I grabbed my axe out of the pack and chopped off green spruce boughs, tossing them onto the moss along with a stack of dry twigs. I pulled off my soaked, freezing mitts and reached into my pocket for the plastic bag containing wooden matches and a striker. My fingers were nearly frozen solid and practically useless, so I tore open the bag with my teeth, held a match between my knuckles and swiped it against the match striker. The match snapped, and then fizzled out. I took a deep breath, trying to stay calm in my desperation. I struck another match, but it didn't flame up either.

The matches had gotten wet, but I tried the remainder of matches anyhow until I came to the last one. I carefully picked it up. *Please God, let it light.* I stroked it smoothly on the striker. It broke in half and fell in the snow. *Now I'm dead—I can't believe this!*

I shoved my frozen hands down my coveralls, between my thighs to thaw. My knees were aching and my legs were stiff. When I felt blood flowing in my fingers, I shoved my icy mitts back on, and took off running down the trail, or maybe it was more like wobbling.

It will take three hours to go back the way I came, but if I cut straight through the forest, I might make it to the road in an hour and find help. I reached in my parka pocket and pulled out a compass and calculated the shortest route through the forest. Sprinting, and stumbling over logs, I ran as fast as I could, but within a few minutes my feet and shins became numb. I stopped and peeled my icy coveralls up to my knees and felt my shins. They were like wooden stubs.

Then I remembered some words of wisdom from an old friend who said, "If you ever get your feet wet and frozen, don't walk on them. Otherwise you'll have to have them amputated. Just make camp, build a huge fire and dry them out before going any farther."

Well, my feet are freezing and I can't build a fire and it's almost dark. A fresh batch of panic coursed through my veins. *What if I crawl? If I crawl I might make it with my feet intact...or I'll just die trying.* I got on my hands and knees and started crawling.

Before long I felt blood flowing to my toes, which was accompanied by the most excruciating pins-and-needles sensation. It moved through my feet, up my ankles and then to my shins. Although it was painful, I was encouraged that

I could feel something again, even if it wasn't pleasant. I was amped. I stood up and took off sprinting through the forest, leaping over logs, and barreled through thick brush like a bull moose. But within 10 minutes my toes and feet went numb again. I decided I should approach the situation by alternating crawling and running—crawl until I regained feeling in my feet, then run like hell until I went numb.

I paused to check the compass. *I should be at the road by now. Am I lost?*

The dark forest closed in around me like a black curtain. I grew weak and stiff. It felt like my system was shutting down and I was ready to call it quits. I started thinking about my folks back home that would be waiting for a Christmas gift, and it wouldn't arrive. I thought about my old hunting beagle, Prince, and how well he chased rabbits, and skillfully turned them toward me. I remembered the taste of mom's special fried rabbit recipe and baked bread. It was so sweet.

Suddenly, I heard a distant sound of a pickup truck. I listened as the engine became louder. *I have to get to the road and flag the truck down!*

After a short 200 yard run, I found myself at the edge of the road. The truck had already sped by, but directly on the other side was a yellow neon sign in the window of a café, glowing as bright as the gates of heaven. I stood up as straight as I could, bowed over with pain and stiffness. I walked across the road, swung open the coffee shop door and met a plume of steam from the café's intense heat. I walked inside past the truck drivers who were seated on the counter stools staring at me, and sat down at the first vacant table.

A waitress hurried over. "Are you alright? What happened to you?"

"I'm fine. Really, I am."

She looked at the water that was starting to drip down my coveralls and onto the floor. Her jaw dropped.

"No, lady, it's not what you think," I explained. "I fell through the ice. I'm just thawing out. Now would you please stop staring at me and give me that pot of coffee?" I knew I wasn't out of the woods yet. I was shivering badly and I was worried about my feet.

I called a friend to bring me some dry clothes, and within four hours I was feeling normal again. Luckily, my battle wounds were minimal—nine missing toenails and a few frost-nipped toes. Not bad for a winter swim in a stinking beaver pond. I have to give credit to my friend whose advice saved my feet from the chopping block.

It has been 30 years since this happened, and there's not a day that goes by when I don't think about it. I often wonder what the outcome would have been if I hadn't said that three word prayer.

CHAPTER 4

Hollywood Misfits

When I realized the purebred Alaskan malamute was the ticket for venturing into the Arctic, I searched for stout, hard working, well-furred malamutes and eventually had 24 dogs in my kennel. They were a mixed bunch of malamutes that other dog mushers didn't want because they trotted too slowly, or they were too large. Most local dog mushers were interested in racing, so they preferred small fast paced dogs. At this time commercial dog sledding tours were becoming popular and since I had such a large family of dogs I decided to give commercial dog sled expeditions a shot.

Everything went well during the first season. I ran dog sledding trips in the Gates of the Arctic National Park and the surrounding area. It is beautiful country and the folks really enjoyed viewing the jagged peaks and traveling on the frozen, winding rivers. I provided the clients with small teams and gave them a short instructional course on dog mushing. The lessons were simple: hang on tightly to the handle bars, don't converse with one another, and just be silent. I explained

One of my wheel dogs, Texas.

that dogs who are trained on verbal command are constantly listening for their instructions. It became clear to me that when the dogs are at work, any unnecessary speaking confuses and distracts them. If they think you are talking to them, but you're not saying anything they can understand, then they don't know what you expect of them. It ruins their confidence and they don't know what to do with themselves. The other lessons were to say "whoa" in a commanding tone when you stop, and "okay" to go.

Sounds simple, right? What I failed to realize at the time was that some adults don't take instruction well, or maybe they just have selective hearing. I watched and listened, trip after trip, to the folks talking to the dogs and conversing amongst themselves incessantly. I had no idea how negatively it was affecting my dogs until the following winter when I hitched up a team of dogs that had been used for the clients' team the previous season. I couldn't believe what I saw! The dogs were jumping around every which way like uncontrollable maniacs, and they didn't listen to my commands whatsoever.

As I got the team going, they settled into their run and started to behave more like themselves—that is, until we started climbing a hill. Typically, hills don't faze a freighting team. It might slow them down but they dig in and power the sled up and over. But, that's not what happened on that particular day. When we got half way up the hill they stopped, turned their heads and looked at me pathetically as if to say, *Okay, we've stopped now, and when you take your foot off the brake we'll go again.*

I was torqued. I realized that many of my clients neglected my dog mushing instructions and totally forgot the most important lesson of all–to give the verbal command to stop when hitting the brakes. If the dogs don't have a verbal command to stop and the musher relies solely on the sled brake, eventually the dogs will learn that when they feel resistance, it means to stop. That doesn't work out too well while freighting heavy loads. You won't get very far, that's for sure.

It took several years to retrain those dogs and build up their shattered confidence after just one season with clients. So, rather than continuing down that frustrating path, I decided to offer dog team supported cross-country skiing expeditions and freighting services with one large team that was capable of hauling thousands of pounds. The one team system worked well. I was in control of the dogs, and my malamutes were spared from turning into insecure wimps that wouldn't pull.

Expeditions can be difficult for some folks who are not used to the arctic wind constantly blistering their faces, and many people just don't have an idea what a true expedition is. Some people just learn to adapt well and deal with the brutal environment. One client told me while we were on an expedition that if you are not humble before you get here, you will be when you leave. I've had some great clients, yet a few of them had it pretty darn rough.

***

After a few years conducting dog sledding expeditions, I stumbled upon an opportunity for the dogs and I to work on the set of Walt Disney's *White Fang*.

It started on a frigid, gray January morning with an unexpected knock on my cabin door. I invited the local dog musher (let's just call him Don) inside, and offered him a chair and a cup of strong, black coffee. After the usual small talk about weather being milder than it used to be, he explained that Disney was searching for a well-trained team of 20 large dogs or Alaskan malamutes for a film project in Haines, Alaska. Don said that they had contacted him, but they thought his huskies were too small. He figured my dogs were exactly what they were looking for and he asked me if I was interested in the job. I jumped at the opportunity.

Don said he would contact the producers and let them know that I was interested, and as a favor he offered to arrange transportation to Haines for me. Within a week, I had my 24 dogs loaded in a U-Haul truck and began the drive down the icy road towards Haines.

When I arrived in Haines, puddles of snow melt covered the streets. Folks were hustling about carrying shopping bags, chatting, and taking pictures. It seemed that everyone was well dressed, even the men were clean shaven and wearing shiny black rubber boots. The town was nothing like I had remembered it when Takhin and I were there seven years earlier. The place seemed to have lost its character. Where were the rough, long-bearded, crooked-nosed fighting loggers, and smelly, hootin' and hollerin' fishermen?

As I looked closer, I recognized many of those clean shaven

gentlemen. I realized they were the tough crowd from back in the day that I had known and liked so well. I figured those fellas were trying to get a job on the movie set, just as I had done, and were busy mingling with the movie cast and crew. But they sure made me feel out of place. I hadn't washed my dirty old jacket all winter. My brown coveralls had a tear at the knee which I had sewn together with dental floss. They smelled like a sled dog harness and were covered in malamute hair. I wasn't exactly wearing my Sunday's best, but usually I'd fit right in at any normal Alaskan town.

I parked the truck at the company's production office, stepped inside and told the receptionist who I was. She was a young gal with a California tan. She greeted me with a bright smile, and then her eyes raked me from my head right down to my grubby dog yard boots. She quickly pulled a map out of her desk with directions scribbled on it and instructed me to transport the dogs 20 miles up the road to a house and property where the dogs and I would be staying. Attached to the map was a paper with a few phone numbers on it, and instructions to set up an appointment to meet the other animal trainers.

The map led me on a winding road rutted in deep snow to a large two story house surrounded with Sitka spruce and cottonwood trees. The property owner was outside loading boxes into his pickup truck as I pulled in. After a handshake and of course some small talk about the mild weather, we walked over to an area shadowed in the trees where 20 dog houses sat in the snow. The area looked like it hadn't been vacant for long. Frozen yellow icicles clung to the sides of each dog house. He explained he had 20 huskies, but he and the dogs moved to a nearby property to give us a place to train without distractions. Apparently, Walt Disney Productions had rented quite a few houses around the Haines area for the cast and crew, so many residents left their homes and took up temporary residence elsewhere.

After offloading my culture shocked, car sick dogs, I drove back into town where I had made an appointment to meet the other animal trainers at a small café. I was starving.

There were a lot of other animals involved in the film and there was a trainer for each one. They even had a fish wrangler to take care of some fish that were in one of the scenes.

I wedged the truck into a parking space at the café and walked inside. The place was packed and if I didn't know better I'd say there was a party going on. People were laughing, smoking, drinking sodas, and showing off the souvenirs they had purchased. I sat down at the only empty table, far in the back corner of the café, pushed aside the ketchup-smeared dishes and kicked the greasy french fry off the bottom of my boot.

When the other animal trainers arrived, they made a beeline for my table as if they knew who I was. I guess it was obvious that I was the other trainer, considering my grungy attire. There were three men and a woman, and they were all very polite and friendly. We sat down and started talking about dogs, bears, wolves and fish that were involved in the film. The waitress passed by a few times, turning her nose up at our dirty little crowd. When she finally came to our table the noise in the place was deafening and had apparently drowned out my request for a broiled steak and baked potato, because all I got was a pile of cold, oily tater tots with a bottle of ketchup. It was a lousy meal and the service was poor, but I reluctantly paid for the meal.

As we got up to leave, the head animal trainer took me by surprise. "Well, Joe thanks for transporting Don's dogs all the way down here to Haines. You heading back home tomorrow or are you planning to stick around town for a few days?"

I was confused, and it took a few seconds before I finally broke the awkward silence. "What the heck are you talking about? These are my dogs, not Don's."

"Don said he hired you to bring his dogs down here."

"Oh bull," I grumbled, getting red in the face as my blood pressure started to rise. "I can't believe this. Are you serious? Don really told you these were *his* dogs?"

"Well, we're paying him for the dogs and you're getting handler's pay. You'd better go get this straightened out with the production office and let me know what the hell's going on. Smells like a skunk to me."

I excused myself from the table and slapped a nickel down for a tip, and drove the rattling U-Haul truck straight to the production office. I stormed through the door and told the California-tanned, smiling receptionist that I was packing up my dogs and going home. She jumped to her feet, and called her boss out of his office.

"What can I do for you, sir?"

"There's something strange going on here and we need to get to the bottom of it or I'm packing up my dogs and getting out of here," I insisted.

"Whoa, you can't just take the dogs and leave. What's the problem?" he questioned. I explained that they'd been duped, and I got screwed, so the dogs and I were going home.

"Come on into my office. Let's get Don on the phone and see what's going on here."

As it turns out, Don's dishonesty got him fired. I, on the other hand, took my rightful place as trainer of my own dogs for the film.

It took a few days for the dust to settle, but it jumpstarted the first of several meetings and pay negotiations. Finally, the issue got resolved and it all worked out. My dogs and I were back in show business.

The actors and trainers were great to work with. The animal trainers had to put in a lot of hours though, probably more than anyone else on the set. One of the basic skills the animals were required to be proficient in was hitting a mark, which basically means they had to be trained to stand on an object on verbal command or by hand signals. The object was usually a small round "mark board" hidden slightly under the snow, or a stick, or a rock on the ground. When an animal can hit a mark reliably, it allows the cameraman to set up the proper camera angle before shooting the scene. I spent quite a few days and nights getting the dogs to hit a mark on command, but within two weeks I had 15 dogs hitting their marks.

I thought we were ready for the opening day of filming until one of the trainers handed me the script and told me to go through it and memorize the actors' lines. That way, I would know when to give commands to the dogs without screwing up the actors' speaking parts. Plus, he informed me that I would be doubling for the part of Alex, so I better remember his entire part. He also instructed that whenever Alex wasn't in the scene and my dogs were, I should be on the set as an extra in case there was a problem. He said it was part of their policy to have the trainer on the scene at all times. It seemed that we animal trainers never had time off.

The filming in Haines lasted a few months, and the dogs did a great job. I was offered an opportunity to continue a career in show business with my malamutes. I wanted to accept the offer in the worst way, but my soul thirsted for the north. It tugged on me the whole time I was in Haines. It was a longing that kept me up at night. It haunted me. I hated it, despised it and wished it would go away, but I longed for the sparking campfires under the night's skies. I missed the northern lights flaring overhead, the malamutes' ancient songs piercing the brutal silence, the challenges of survival, the freedom of breaking trail, traveling, and camping wherever I wished. I ached for the exhilaration of exploring God's creation. I was hopelessly hooked.

I declined the once-in-a-lifetime offer. Instead I'd go north, shovel dog poop every summer and see where the trail led. Only God knew where that decision would take me, but I was used to living in blind faith, venturing into the unknown. I figured

On the set of White Fang.

Me (sitting on the sled) doubling for the part of Alex with my team pulling the sled.

someday I'd look back on that decision not to do the Hollywood thing and either kick myself very hard or be thankful I didn't accept the offer. It was a rocky and rough trail that I followed, and several years later I found myself on another adventure when I decided to leave Coldfoot.

Coldfoot had lost its spirit. The old timers had passed on, and low gold prices drove the other gold miners out of the area. The most noticeable change was the new gang in town, government regulators. They were zealous fanatics that descended on local business owners and gold miners with new laws and regulations. They treated everyone as if they were criminals even though most folks were upstanding, law abiding citizens. The regulators were heavily armed with assault weapons and traveled the countryside on ATV's, airplanes, and helicopters, while spending millions of dollars of tax payers' money searching for citizens committing regulatory infractions. They built a multi-million dollar fortress a few miles from Coldfoot, spoiling the once wild, pristine wilderness and transforming it to a city park atmosphere with designated hiking trails, permit processes and increased patrols of air and land traffic.

The Park Service employees were the worst and became a major obstacle for me as they tried to regulate my commercial dog sledding expeditions. As they cruised the countryside on loud, smoking, stinking snowmobiles collecting and analyzing dog feces (which they claimed was harmful to the environment) they attempted to shut down my business. Their study of dog feces as an environmental hazard was eventually found to be "inconclusive," but it gave me a sour taste of what was coming. Restricted freedom has always been my pet peeve. It is the spirit of America. A free country is successful only with common sense laws being strictly enforced, but over-regulation can get to the point where every citizen is a criminal whether they know it or not. I grew tired of being hassled every time my malamutes left frozen crap on the tundra.

I chose this over Hollywood.

So, I decided to go farther north where it was still a free country and I didn't have to concern myself with bureaucrats following me around collecting my malamutes' poop.

CHAPTER 5

Hendersonville: Population 1

Several years later I accepted the job of manager at a remote camp in the Arctic which was used as a base location for hunters, scientific researchers, and drilling crews. It was located in the foothills of the Brooks Range, about 40 miles south of the Arctic Ocean. This place was exactly what I had been looking for, but it was incredibly remote. There were no roads to the camp, so it could only be accessed via air taxi services. Needless to say, it was a logistical challenge to get me and my 26 dogs to the camp. I needed to hire a highly skilled pilot who was experienced and comfortable flying in the Arctic in all sorts of weather conditions.

That's when I met Dirk and Danielle, whom own and operate Coyote Air Service based in Coldfoot. It is a family owned business which provides bush service in the Arctic. I admired Dirk and his aviation skills. He had a reputation as the one of the best bush pilots in the area.

It was May and spring was in the air when Dirk and I loaded seven of the dogs, groceries, dog food, and personal items in the plane, and climbed aboard. Dirk fired up the engine and we sped down the airstrip leaving a trail of dust behind us. As I watched Coldfoot disappear behind me I knew I had made the right decision to leave that area. The plane followed the winding, ice-choked Koyukuk River, and passed over the village of Wiseman where I spotted my old log cabin. The village looked small and insignificant compared to the valleys and mountains enveloping it and I thought, *It's a shame I didn't have more time to explore this area as much as I would have liked to, but it's time to move on.*

Dirk's voice came over the headset. He told me the pass was clear of fog and it would take around three hours to get to the camp. I nodded, and pressed against the window to take in the scenery passing below us. As far as I could see in every direction were jagged, gray limestone peaks, some of which were covered in snow while others were wind torn and bare. Dall sheep stood on cliffs with their newborn lambs while large golden eagles circled above, and to the north, the rugged mountain peaks scraped the clouds.

The plane continued a slow ascent following a river that flowed between two jagged pinnacles until we crested the summit. It seemed we had passed through the gates of spring and into winter. The tundra was covered in deep snow and the rivers were still frozen. Thousands of caribou were migrating on the mountainsides. From the air the caribou looked like army ants on the march.

As Dirk flew down another winding river the mountains fell away to gentle rolling hills. He raised his arm and pointed ahead into the distance at a series of bright orange trailers that stuck out like a sore thumb against the white landscape. *This is it? Holy smokes! This is literally in the middle of nowhere. It's perfect!*

The airstrip was blown clear of snow and Dirk skillfully landed the plane, taxied close to one of the buildings and came to a stop. Some of the trailers were completely drifted over with snow, but the first one we came to with an accessible door became my personal bunkhouse.

We quickly offloaded the anxious dogs. They were relieved

to stretch their legs and sniff around their new home. While I picketed the dogs on chains, Dirk offloaded my supplies and said he'd be back the next day with another load of groceries and the rest of the dogs. Wasting no time, he climbed back into the plane and departed before the evening fog rolled in from the Arctic Ocean.

As the sounds of Dirk's plane faded into the distance, I packed my gear into the trailer, and began exploring around my new home. The camp was very small with a dozen bunkhouse trailers organized in several rows. Adjacent to the trailers were three large dome-shaped tents. The tents were each about the size of a four car garage, constructed with heavy insulated vinyl material that could withstand hurricane-force winds and heavy snowfall. One of the tents had a huge hole torn through the wall, probably the work of a grizzly bear, and had obviously been used as a place to store trash and other random items. It was piled high with moldy mattresses, kitchen equipment, dishes, fuel drums, and tools.

Another tent housed a rickety diesel generator that provided electricity for the camp, but after a brief inspection it was obvious that it needed some major repairs before it would run again. In the third tent, farthest from the airstrip, I found the kitchen and dining hall area complete with tables and chairs, a coffee maker, and a colony of chattering ground squirrels.

Behind the bunkhouse trailers were two outhouses. The men's outhouse was painted dark blue and had a stack of old, worn out Field & Stream magazines inside. The women's outhouse was Pepto-Bismol pink. It was equipped with a sky light and there were sun-faded artificial flowers planted in the gravel outside the door. Not very far beyond the outhouses was a junk yard with discarded lumber, trash, more rusty oil drums, and a twisted airplane wing.

After assessing the camp, I realized I had been misinformed about the condition of the place, but I didn't mind the extra

The women's outhouse at the camp, filled with hard packed snow after a windstorm.

work and repairs to get things up and running. Heck, I was in the Arctic and as far as I was concerned, just being there was luxurious enough.

As the days went by, I cherished being there more and more. I made repairs to the trailers, got the generator in working order, cleaned the trash heap in the tent, and got rid of the ground squirrels that had taken up residence in the dining hall over the winter. Once it was cleaned up and organized, it was a comfortable place to live.

The camp was unique in that it had modern conveniences, and yet it was isolated in the arctic wilderness, surrounded by such diverse and abundant wildlife. Sometimes caribou wandered between the trailers and on the airstrip and geese would settle in the grass next to the trailers, cackling as they soaked up the sun's warmth. Once in a while a grizzly bear would walk through camp, and almost every day red foxes could be seen roaming the hills, chasing ground squirrels or lemmings while falcons darted overhead, preying on the ptarmigan at the river's edge. The river was crystal clear and flowed gently over smooth boulders. Occasionally an arctic grayling would break the surface.

I always enjoyed watching caribou graze while the calves chased each other around like little children playing tag on the playground. They seemed to live a carefree life, but come July their world changes. Clouds of blood-thirsty mosquitoes tormented them. I remember watching an old bull reach his breaking point and sprint across the wet tundra bucking, shaking, and kicking like a wild horse until he collapsed with exhaustion. Caribou are the toughest animals that I've ever seen. How they have survived thousands of years in the brutal arctic environment is a testament of their toughness. Without caribou, the wolves, wolverines, bears, and ravens would suffer since caribou meat is their staple. They are the lifeblood of the Arctic and after residing at the camp for several months caribou meat became my main fare also. I always enjoyed hunting them.

***

I remember one August day, I spotted a huge bull caribou alongside a creek in the distance. His antlers stood above the tall willows and his long, white cape waved in the breeze. He was an impressive animal with a broad chest, and his ribs were smooth, covered in a layer of fat. I was relieved to see him since I hadn't seen any caribou for several months and I relied on their meat for survival. The bull walked cautiously and slowly along the brushy creek, glancing periodically at a small herd of cow caribou that lay on the hillside. It was too far for a shot, around 800 yards, so I slung my rifle over my shoulder and worked my way across the tundra toward him. He was oblivious to my approach. In the thick brush I caught glimpses of his antlers slowly bobbing up and down as he grazed. His antlers looked like oak tree branches and had strips of velvet hanging from them. As I crept deeper in the willows, I lost sight of his antlers but kept moving toward him.

I heard a loud grunt that sounded like he was right beside me. I kneeled down and pushed aside the shrubs with the barrel of my rifle. He was so close I could hear him chewing his cud. Finally I caught a glimpse of him, but I couldn't get a clean shot. If I stayed there too long, he would catch my scent and run away, taking the cows with him. That was the last thing I wanted. I needed those cows to stay in the valley to attract more bulls. I figured I would need at least five bulls to give me enough to subsist on for the winter.

I decided to walk back to a small hill that I had passed by earlier rather than hang around there and scare him away. From the vantage point of the hill, I was confident that I would have a good shot. I quietly worked my way out of the bushes and when I arrived at the top of the hill I could see the bull clearly. I lay on my stomach with my elbows resting on the moss and firmly held the rifle.

I found the caribou through the scope. He stood broadside and looked strong and confident as he swung his massive antlers over his back and raised his muzzle upward checking the wind. I watched him lower his head for a moment, and when he raised it there were blades of grass hanging from his mouth. He swung around, eyeing the cows that were now walking along a distant hillside feeding on moss. I estimated the bull was about 650 yards away.

The earthy fragrance of lichen filled my lungs as I inhaled deeply and held my breath. I held the crosshairs over his shoulder a few inches above his back to allow for the bullet to drop, and held steady. I squeezed the trigger, and the shot rang in my ears. The caribou dropped and disappeared in the vegetation, except for his antlers, which stood in plain view.

Thank God! I stood up and started hiking across the tundra toward my harvest as I slung my rifle over my shoulder. I worked my way through the thick arctic flora, ducking under the gnarled willow branches, practically crawling. I heard brush rustling behind me. With a rush of adrenaline, I whipped around with my rifle barrel aimed from the hip, ready to shoot. I couldn't see a thing through the thick bushes, but I could smell the unmistakable stench of a grizzly bear. I heard a low, guttural growl that caused the hair on my neck to stand up and a cold sweat to come over me. I stood there very still, holding my breath, with a death grip on my rifle. My senses were tuned to the slightest movements in the brush, but everything was still and my surroundings fell silent. I just knew a grizzly was stalking me, slithering around in the thick brush waiting for an opportunity to ambush, but I'd had my fair share of those bastards charge me and I wasn't taking any chances. I kept my finger on the trigger and slowly, very slowly, inched closer toward the caribou.

I came upon the creek and straight across it lay the caribou on a small patch of lush grass surrounded by thick brush. To my surprise, there were two caribou lying dead, side by side. In the past, I had killed two caribou with a single bullet when I shot at two standing next to each other, but never had I killed two at once on accident. It was surreal.

I identified the caribou that I had intended to shoot from his majestic set of antlers. The second caribou lay on his stomach in an odd position with his legs tucked under him, his head resting on the tundra and his antlers standing straight up toward the blue sky. He had a very distinct, unique set of antlers that branched out wide with a double shovel that nearly rubbed against his snout, but his left brow tine pointed down like a large fang over his eye. His left eye was closed and he was very still, convincing me he was dead. The creek that separated us was narrow and deep, but not narrow enough to risk jumping

Self portrait after a caribou harvest.

across, so I searched upstream for a good place to cross, and then worked my way toward the two dead caribou.

The day was starting to warm up, my legs were sweating under my rubber hip waders and mosquitoes were chewing my ears. I hustled my pace through the bushes to get away from the bugs and nearly tripped over one of the caribou. As I regained my footing and studied the kill site, I realized that the other caribou was missing. The caribou with the unique set of antlers was gone. I figured the grizzly bear dragged him away while I was busy trying to cross the creek. Bears had stolen my caribou a time or two before, and I was getting fed up with it. I placed my pack board and skinning knives beside the dead bull and searched for bear tracks or a blood trail, but there were none.

After a half hour of searching the area I gave up and went to work field dressing the bull, feeling nervous with my back turned to the brush. I gutted and skinned the caribou, rinsed the heart in the creek, and set it on the moss beside the water so I wouldn't forget to grab it on my way back to camp. After quartering the caribou and rolling the hide up in a bundle and tying it, I washed the blood off my hands started relaying the quarters down the creek to a small, open meadow where I felt safer leaving the meat as I packed one piece at a time back to the camp.

I quickly walked back to the caribou for another load of meat. Right away, I noticed the heart was gone. Imprinted deep in the mud were large bear tracks. I estimated he was around 500 lbs.

As I packed the rest of the meat to the meadow, I wondered, why *the bear would steal the heart if he had already stolen the other caribou. Didn't he already get enough?* It didn't make sense to me. *And why wasn't there a pool of blood where the other caribou lay? Maybe he wasn't dead.*

That evening I hung up the quartered meat from the ridge poles in the smokehouse and lit a smudge fire under it to keep the flies away. I laid out the caribou hide and salted it. I sliced a thick steak from the hind quarter and went to my bunk for dinner.

As the steak sizzled in the skillet, I looked out the window to the north and saw snow clouds rolling in from the Arctic Ocean. *That's excellent,* I thought. *It'll be so much easier to track that bear if it snows.*

Around midnight, the dogs woke me with alarming growling and barking. Right away I knew it was the bear. I grabbed my rifle and flashlight and ran out the door full speed ahead toward the smokehouse. When I got there, a bear-sized hole was torn through the screen wall. I cautiously stepped through it, prepared to shoot the first thing that moved. I shined the light inside. The bear wasn't there, but the meat was swinging back and forth on the ropes and one quarter was missing.

As I swung open the trailer door a few snowflakes fell before the light. I was glad to see it snowing and I couldn't wait until morning to track down the bear.

Morning finally arrived with a fresh layer of snow on the tundra. I got dressed in a hurry, grabbed my rifle and rushed out across the white landscape to the hill from which I had shot the caribou. As I searched the tundra with my binoculars, I saw something dark moving in the tall willows a half mile up the creek. I lowered my binoculars and headed toward it with determination.

The skies were clear and there was cold breeze on my face. Ankle-deep snow muffled the sounds of my footsteps as I approached the animal. When I got closer I heard some sticks snap. *Now it's my turn to ambush you, you thieving bear.* Then it wandered into view. It was a caribou, the same one that I thought I had killed and the bear had stolen. His left eye was missing. He walked straight toward me and stopped 20 feet away. His ears perked up, twitching nervously. He turned his head cautiously side to side. Then he lowered himself until his chin rested on the snow and lay perfectly still in the same position I found him in the previous day, looking just as dead as ever.

***

Subsisting on a caribou meat diet was a very healthy lifestyle, but there are tricks to the trade that I had learned when I lived in Northern British Columbia. That's where I met a kind, and wise gentleman named Charlie.

Charlie belonged to the Carrier Indian Tribe in Canada. He grew up at a time when men and women survived from their harvests of game animals and fish. I never did know Charlie's exact age and he didn't know either, but evidence from his stories suggested he was in his late 80's early 90's. I remember he had mentioned seeing his first white man when he was a small child during the gold rush.

"There were hundreds of them on the Grease Trail walking toward us, bowed over with heavy packs, and talking a gibberish language," he recalled.

It must have been frightening for Charlie to see all those strange men invading his land in pursuit of a yellow rock that they called "gold."

Charlie's tribe engaged in trade with coastal Indians along trails known as Grease Trails. In exchange for their hides— usually beaver, pine marten and lynx furs—they acquired grease, which was actually oil extracted from eulachon (commonly referred to as candlefish). The oil was an important addition to their diet, which consisted primarily of lean moose meat.

When I asked Charlie about his hunting experiences, his only eye gleamed with pride and became misty. Charlie's left eye was sewn shut and a scar ran from his forehead, through his left brow and down his cheek. I never asked him how he lost his eye and got that horrible scar, but wish I had. His face was dark, leathery and weathered with wrinkles, deeper wrinkles than I had ever seen before. Many nights, Charlie and I sat beside his wood burning stove drinking black coffee and talking about his life in the bush. Moose hunting was a frequent topic.

Although Charlie was in very good physical condition considering his age, he had difficulties packing moose meat on his back, which was essentially the only way to transfer the meat from the kill sight to his home. Needless to say, he didn't hunt any longer, but he still savored the taste of fresh moose roasted over a crackling fire. When Charlie's supply of moose meat ran low he would reveal one of his secret hunting areas to me. So, he and I always had plenty of moose meat, and it was my main staple for breakfast, lunch, and dinner.

After several months living off moose meat and little else, I

Charlie. (sketch by Daryl Griffin)

started to feel weak. It didn't matter how much I ate, it seemed I just grew hungrier and weaker. One night, I mentioned to Charlie how sick I felt. He told me to go and talk with the shaman. A few days later, when I couldn't take the bloated feeling any longer, I did just that.

The shaman lived in a small log cabin just outside the village. I knocked softly on the door, expecting to see an old man on the other side. Instead, an elderly lady pulled the squeaky door open and shot me a friendly, toothless smile.

I explained to her my ailment. Without saying a word, she nodded her head as she shuffled over to the kitchen cabinet and pulled out two jars filled with an orange-red liquid and handed them to me. She scolded me and informed me that I should "always dip meat in the salmon oil."

I examined the jars and thanked her graciously. She grinned and shook her head with amused condescension and said, "Crazy white man! You bring back those jars when they're finished and I'll have more for you."

"Yes, ma'am, I certainly will. It might be a while, but I'll be back. Thank you."

After I dipped the moose meat in oil before eating it, in a few days I felt fine. Now, when I slice off a lean caribou or moose steak, I remember Charlie's Grease Trail story and the shaman's advice for a crazy white man.

CHAPTER 6

Project Leffingwell Expeditions

The camp was a busy place during summer and fall. It was a hub for pilots, scientists, and hunters. Although I spent a lot of time hunting and fishing, there was plenty of work to do otherwise, like maintaining the generators, fueling aircrafts, and cooking for guests. I didn't mind fueling helicopters and airplanes, but flipping burgers and cooking wasn't my forte. Most of my guests were hunters or geologists and they weren't fussy about their meals—or maybe they were, but they didn't complain. Rather than serve an extravagant meal, I made it easy on myself and grilled steaks for breakfast and dinner. It was simple and the guests always loved it. Every so often I added fried caribou brains with scrambled eggs to the breakfast menu just to spice things up a bit. Most of the folks liked it, but there were a few who didn't. I recall one clean cut, frail looking gentleman who seemed to enjoy his breakfast, and when I offered him seconds he stood right up and reached across the table for more. But when his hunting partners told him he had just had eaten eggs with fried caribou brains he turned pale as a ghost and ran out of the dining hall.

The place had a relaxed, upbeat atmosphere and in the evenings the dining hall turned into an interesting hangout, a gathering place of people from different walks of life, with

Lake trout caught with a fly rod.

differing views and theories about oil exploration in the Arctic, hunting, and tourism. The environmentalists despised oil drilling, and flew around in fuel guzzling helicopters taking photographs of the drill rigs, while field scientists bowed over their laptops, sipping wine and entering information into their database. The hunters guzzled beer and cleverly told stories that made themselves look like Grizzly Adams, and tourists sat around complaining about summer snow storms and mosquitoes that sucked their blood dry.

There was always interesting literature and propaganda strewn on the tables that folks left behind. One day, as I thumbed through the pages of a geological publication, I came across an excerpt from an old newspaper dating back to 1907 stating:

Leffingwell and two other members of his party had left the ship in February with 60 days' provisions for the supposed continent north of Alaska's Arctic coast. They have been gone for 70 days. One of their dog teams had returned but it's feared the three men had met death in the frozen north.

A black and white photo showed three men sitting on a gnarled chunk of sea ice. They were dressed in caribou fur clothing and a handsome Alaskan malamute stood proudly at their side.

I had never seen that particular photo before, nor had I heard the story of this expedition, which came as a surprise because I thought I had read every Arctic explorer book printed. As a kid, I would scour the library shelves for books about Arctic explorers. When I found one that I hadn't yet read, it was like discovering a hidden treasure. Etched in my memory were several photographs of early 20th century explorers—Scott, Peary and Cook—proudly standing by their country's flags with looks of triumph and travail. Their blistered faces and their empty eyes looked as if they had just seen hell. I was fascinated by their stories of adventure and the tragic endings that had claimed some of these great men. I was blown away and horrified at some of the circumstances these explorers found themselves in, like having to eat their beloved dogs in hopes of staying alive long enough to set foot in their homeland again.

One of the men in the journal photo was geologist and explorer, Ernest de Koven Leffingwell (1875-1971), and his story intrigued me. Contrary to the excerpt in the article, Leffingwell and his party hadn't perished, and actually they had fared relatively well.

The Duchess of Bedford frozen in the Beaufort Sea. (photo courtesy of the U.S. Geological Survey Photographic Library)

Leffingwell's expedition, known as the Anglo-American Polar Expedition, departed from San Francisco on May 22, 1906, in a sealing schooner called the Duchess of Bedford. The expedition's purpose was to verify land believed to exist north of Alaska's Arctic coast. When the Duchess of Bedford became ice-bound near Flaxman Island off the Arctic coast, Leffingwell, ship captain Ejnar Mikkelson, and the other crew members wintered over.

The following spring, it became evident that the ship was damaged beyond repair and no longer seaworthy. The Anglo-American Polar Expedition was effectively over, and most of the crew returned home via whaling vessel. Leffingwell and Mikkelson, however, stayed behind. Using salvaged material from the wrecked ship, they built a cabin and later that year, Mikkelson went home.

Leffingwell, on the other hand, stayed behind until 1914, and with the help of a few local Inupiat assistants, he surveyed and mapped the land and studied Alaska's arctic environment. When he returned to civilization, he published his findings in a U.S. Geological Survey publication.

Leffingwell had traveled over 4,500 miles by dog team or small boat and mapped the Arctic coastline between Point Barrow and the Canadian border. Additionally, he mapped the geographic and geologic features of approximately 4,000 square miles of mainland, known in modern times as the Arctic National Wildlife Refuge (ANWR). He was the first to accurately predict the presence of oil at what is now one of the largest oil fields in North America at Prudhoe Bay. These are just a few of his accomplishments, however, his work received little recognition and he did not fail to notice the lack of attention.

Leffingwell once stated, "Not being spectacular attracted little public notice, and during the excitement caused by Peary, Cook, Stefansson, and Amundsen, I was the forgotten man."

Leffingwell never sought fame, prestige or wide recognition

Ernest de Koven Leffingwell. (photo courtesy of the U.S. Geological Survey Photographic Library)

for his extraordinary achievements. The media at the time must have operated much like they do currently, highlighting certain individuals and making them out to be heroes while ignoring people who are worthy of recognition.   It always seemed backwards to me. Somehow, the guy who ends up losing his fingers to frostbite or narrowly escaping death for one reason or another is always viewed as the hero, but the one who comes back unscathed is ignored. It seems like the one who runs into the least trouble is probably the most experienced and skilled. Most likely, this was the case with Leffingwell. It is a shame he was never viewed as a hero for his remarkable contributions.

His story fascinated me, so I decided to research his work further and sought out a copy of his U.S. Geological Survey report as well as his personal journal. According to Leffingwell's journal, the camp I was managing was located approximately 60 miles south of his old cabin on Flaxman Island. This really intrigued me. I wanted nothing more than see the rugged landscape that he had described in his publication and to find his cabin. I gathered as much information about Leffingwell's expedition as I could and decided to engineer a plan to follow his route by dog team. I would call it the Project Leffingwell Expedition.

I knew that retracing Leffingwell's route was a major undertaking. I estimated that it would take a year to coordinate the logistics and at least three winters to complete the project. The plan was to work at the camp during the summer months and be out with the team on the expedition for the seven months of winter for three seasons. I would have to take care of all the gear and food preparations myself with limited resources.

Needless to say, I had a huge responsibility to myself and the dogs to ensure that we had enough food and supplies to make it through the duration of the expedition. All dog food for the entire seven months of winter had to be flown in from the closest feed store 500 miles away before the camp's airstrip was closed for winter in early October. I planned to keep my diet simple, relying on a menu of meat, fish, muktuk and caribou tallow.

I wasted no time getting started with preparations, so between maintaining the camp and flipping burgers for guests, I took time to harvest caribou, tan the skins, and sew them into parkas, mukluks, and mitts. I designed a simple canvas tent

The tent I designed to withstand high winds has been my only shelter for many winters.

that could withstand high winds and purchased a small tent stove in which I could burn willows as my main source of heat and cooking fuel. I built three toboggan-style freight sleds, which I planned to tie together in tandem behind the team for the expedition.

I had a couple of routes in mind. I wanted to cover a large portion of Leffingwell's route, but I also wanted to explore some areas that had sparked a personal interest, mostly because of the challenging terrain.

Drawing on experiences from my previous expeditions in the mountains, I knew the project would require the largest team possible to haul our supply of rations. There would be obstacles to deal with on a daily basis, like waist deep snow and steep mountain passes that only a very large and powerful team can ascend.

I used that first winter at the camp to train all 25 malamutes to work together as one team and teach the lead dogs to negotiate the vast, windblown tundra during white-outs. By trial and error, I devised a hitch system for the team that was more efficient than the standard tandem rig or fan hitch.

I spent the following summer managing the camp and eagerly anticipating the expedition. I made sure to harvest enough caribou meat and fish to subsist on the long months of winter.

Finally, in mid November the Project Leffingwell Expedition was set to commence. The dogs were muscled up and rearing to go. Deep snow covered the tundra and the rivers were frozen, but there was one fuzzy little hitch in my plans. A tiny red and white puppy, the sole offspring of one of my young females, was born just a few days before we were scheduled to depart on the expedition. She was a healthy and lively gal, but I knew I would have to postpone the expedition for a short while.

Ten days later, I felt confident that the puppy was strong enough to be away from her mother for most of the day as we traveled. I wrapped the little pup in a soft caribou calfskin and placed her in a wooden box which I tucked inside one of the sleds. And with that, we were on our way.

It was a relief to finally be breaking trail on the expedition after a year of tedious preparation, but at the same time it felt strange not knowing what lay ahead for me and the team for the next five months. I had to rely completely on my dogs and trust in God for my survival. I was at the mercy of one of the most brutal environments on earth where temperatures could reach -100°F with the wind chill, crevasses lay hidden on mountain sides, and thin ice awaited on rivers. Many of the areas that I had planned to explore were exceedingly rugged. They were places where dog teams hadn't traveled since Leffingwell broke trail there with his malamutes 100 years prior. If I got into trouble, it would be nearly impossible for us to be rescued. There wasn't a person on this planet that knew where I was, except for me, and although I was carrying an analog phone it wasn't exactly a reliable means of communication with the civilized world.

Wrapped snug and tight in her caribou skins, the puppy fared well and grew amazingly fat and strong during the first month of the expedition. Every night after traveling, I set up camp and staked out the dogs on picket lines, but the pup's mother was given a special spot amongst the willows, protecting her from the menacing wind. Once mom dug through the snow and made a nest on the soft tundra, I placed the pup next to her tummy where she could nurse and keep warm.

By Christmas she was weaned from mom and was a fat little gal, romping, chewing and playing with all the other dogs, especially Major, a young male with a plush black and white coat. Every night the puppy would wander out of her mom's nest and tuck close against to Major's thick fur.

Two days before Christmas, the puppy didn't seem to be her peppy self anymore. She was getting awfully weak, so I brought her inside my tent and tried feeding her, but she refused to eat.

I knew the little pup would never see the mountains, travel across the tundra, or curl up and feel the warmth of Major again, unless she ate immediately. Cutting small pieces of raw meat I forced fed the pup. The next morning, the puppy still looked weak and frail as she lay next to me on the sleeping bag. I fired up the woodstove, placed a pot of snow on it to melt for water, and pulled a piece of frozen meat out of my food pouch and set it under the stove to thaw. As I went outside to gather more firewood, I took the pup out to be with her mother.

When I returned, I kicked off my snowshoes and dropped the wood by my tent. I noticed tiny paw prints going under the tent door. I unzipped and opened the door to find that the puppy had knocked over the water and eaten the meat I'd left

Major and Little Savage.

out to thaw, which was intended to be my breakfast.

"You little savage!" I grumbled. She lay there with a tummy as rounds as a balloon, and she seemed to be smiling. The blood from the meat had stained the sides of her mouth like a clown in a circus. After a few days, Little Savage grew stronger and more robust than ever.

During that first winter of the Project Leffingwell Expedition, the team and I covered a large portion of the route in the mountains. The conditions were harsh, with very little snow, high winds, and a lot of blizzards, but the malamutes thrived in the environment.

A typical day consisted of tearing down camp, breaking trail for five to eight hours, setting up camp, feeding the dogs, strapping on my snowshoes and scouting a route for the next day. We covered a lot of ground, but during the dead of winter when the sun never rises in the Arctic for 72 consecutive days, progress was slow because of the dangers of crevasses and cliffs hidden in the darkness.

Many of the places I selected as camp sites were locations where Leffingwell had camped. They were the most inviting places to settle in for the night, given their abundant firewood. We made our way off the northern flank of the Brooks Range, across the flats of arctic tundra, and the dogs finally set their big paws on the smooth ice of the Beaufort Sea. We were getting closer to Leffingwell's cabin.

We mushed several miles out on the sea taking advantage of the smooth ice and a stout wind at our backs that pushed us along. As darkness settled on us, we headed inland. However, along with darkness, a blizzard found us and blinded our view of the shore where we had planned to camp for the night. Between the shoreline and us was a barrage of head-high, knee-busting, paw-piercing icebergs. I am sure Mother Nature has a sense of humor, but I couldn't find it in myself to laugh about the barricade of ice. We had no choice, we had to get to land and wait out the windstorm that was salivating to get to us. So the dogs went right to work busting their way over the jumbled and twisted ice.

After muscling through the obstacle, we came to a halt on the beach next to a large driftwood log. It looked like a good place to dig in for the night. I pulled the tent out of the sled, set it up alongside the log and fed the dogs. That night the blizzard came in full blast, throwing dry, sandy snow over the log and against the side of the tent.

From inside of the tent, the sound of the wind was deafening. The blizzard was having her way, shaking and hammering the canvas, but I managed to get the wood stove burning. In the midst of an outright savage environment, the tent was no longer a piece of cold, white canvas, but was transformed into a comfortable, warm and hospitable abode. Being in the Arctic, particularly during a bad storm, conjures up a whole new appreciation for the simple things in life that are so easily taken for granted, like food and shelter.

The following morning brought an unusual silence. The wind had died and the malamutes' lively morning howl sounded muffled. The blizzard had enveloped my tent in hard packed snow. To get out, I punched an opening through the snowdrift with my fist towards the top of the door, wiggled out, and slid down the drift. The dogs were quite impressed as they watched me squeeze out of that hole like a contortionist. Standing up, I scanned the landscape to get an idea of where we were. Nothing looked familiar. There were no landmarks or hills, just flat terrain with wheat brown grass protruding through the snow.

On the horizon I noticed a strange object, something that didn't belong. It resembled a boat. *Why would a boat be lying out in the middle of the tundra*, I thought. Curiosity grabbed me and I headed off in a trot toward the boat. As I approached it, I realized it was the remnants of a cabin. But, the cabin I had been looking for was on an island. *Surely the wind didn't push us offshore so far that we landed on an island. How could I have made such a complete navigational blunder?* Taking a closer look at the old structure, and the few walls that were standing, I realized this was it—I was standing on Leffingwell's cabin doorsteps.

I had to take back the hundred times I cussed the blistering wind, and be thankful she drove us off course, causing us to find the cabin where Leffingwell started his historic expeditions. What a coincidence we found our way through a cursed blizzard, over 50 miles of sea ice, and through a pinnacled barrier of icebergs, to a cabin on an island built 100 years ago. One of the things that Leffingwell had salvaged from the ship that I recognized from old photos was a large steel water tank. There it lay beside the dilapidated cabin along with scraps of lumber, dog sled runners, and other ship material neatly stacked as if Leffingwell had every intention to come back and resume his explorations.

As I stood on Leffingwell's old doorsteps, it gave me a new perspective of the magnitude of his expedition. He must have felt quite small in comparison to the vast Arctic, knowing how easy it was to get lost, as so many other explorers had.

We camped near Leffingwell's cabin for a couple of days, and then on a clear, calm morning the team and I hit the trail again. I noticed Hooch, one of the wheel dogs, was getting bored and tired. So I put him in lead alongside Bear and Angel to give him a break. Hooch's tall 115 lb stature looked comical next to the smaller leaders, but once in a while I put a wheel dog in lead. It works wonders for their outlook on life. Boy, he must have felt as though he had just discovered the North Pole! He proudly curled his tail so tight I thought it might break in two. He was ecstatic leading his comrades across the ice.

As the team trotted behind their new leader, Bear spotted a dark object on the horizon and bolted towards it. His excitement migrated down the gangline energizing all the dogs. As we came closer, the object started to take shape. It looked like a tripod. We pulled up to the 20 foot tall tower which was constructed with driftwood logs. I examined the axe marks on the logs and noticed lichen growing on the base of the tripod. I figured it was about 100 years old. In Leffingwell's journal, he had mentioned building a triangulation tower for his survey at about this location. I was thrilled to have found it.

By April, the sun's warmth started melting the snow and rivers were opening up. I was reluctant to call it quits, but I knew the time had come to end the expedition and head back to the camp. The dogs were in great spirits as they had been for the entire five months and Little Savage had grown handsomely large and healthy. She spent the last two months trailing behind the team, playing with lemmings and chasing

What's left of Leffingwell's cabin. My freighting team in the background.

Leffingwell's cabin in the early 1900's. (photo courtesy of the U.S. Geological Survey Photographic Library)

ptarmigan, but once in a while she would get tired, and hop on the sleds for a ride.

I arrived at the camp at the end of April and went back to work flipping burgers, maintaining camp generators, fueling aircrafts, taking care of guests, and preparing for the following expedition season.

CHAPTER 7

Culture Shock

One summer I met a lovely geologist, Andrea, who would eventually become my wife, but first I had to move back to civilization and that was more difficult than it sounds. I had 25 malamutes, sleds gear and all my worldly belongings at the camp. Everything had to be transported to Deadhorse, and then shipped by truck 500 miles to Fairbanks. It was a logistical challenge and a nightmare to say the least.

The following winter, I set out with the team for another expedition and at the end of the season we ended up in Deadhorse where we met up with Andrea, who had driven up the Dalton Highway with a pickup truck and trailer. We hired a trucking company to transport the sleds and gear for us and loaded all the dogs in the truck and trailer. Everything went smoothly—that is, until the transmission blew out at the top of the steepest, curviest part of the highway aside from Atigun Pass. I couldn't believe it! There we were with 25 malamutes cluelessly drooling in the back of the truck, enjoying their first ride in a vehicle in over three years (for some of them it was their first ride ever), and we were on the verge of careening off a cliff to our demise. I did my best not to burn out the brakes trying to maintain control of my speed and negotiate the curves. By the time we got to the pull out area at the bottom of

Andrea holding Farmer as a pup.

Andrea and I hunting caribou.

the hill, the brakes were smoking but I pulled over and threw some snow on them. All the while, Andrea was awfully quiet.

It was a white knuckle ride, which goes without saying. We flagged down a big rig driver. He was a very kind gentleman whom offered to tow us back up the hill and load our truck onto his flatbed trailer at a road maintenance camp. A few hours later the truck, trailer and all the dogs were loaded, and we climbed into the truck with the driver and rode safely down the potholed highway all the way to Fairbanks.

When we arrived in Fairbanks, I was shocked at how large the city had grown since the last time I'd been there. Fairbanks was bustling with activity and construction. Green, forested areas that used to be the outskirts of town were now populated by chain restaurants and box stores.

With the help of a friend we got the pickup offloaded and Andrea and I settled into our home outside of Fairbanks in a community called Two Rivers. During the summer and fall I worked in Fairbanks as a heavy duty mechanic and on weekends we spent our spare time fly fishing like there was no tomorrow.

When winter arrived, I started preparing for the upcoming expedition season. Dog sledding in the Two Rivers area wasn't the same as the Arctic where I could travel for the entire winter without seeing another human being. Now, I had groomed trails to train on, and speedy racing teams to share them with. Most of the mushers that I met on the trails were friendly, but a few of them gave me dirty looks as they whizzed past me. I guess my dogs were too big and hogging the trail.

The trails were narrow and my malamutes had no idea how to pass oncoming teams. When a team approached, I could hear the musher shouting, "On by! On by!" But I didn't know how my big dogs would react to sharing the trail with others, so in a panic I'd drag them off the trail and let the speedsters try to pass by, but every time a team would get right up to us, the leaders would stop and the rest of the team would crumple up behind them in a tangled mess. Of course, the musher was always upset with me and blamed us for frightening their dogs and causing the mess.

On one training run when a team approached us head on, I stopped my team, stomped in the snow hook and stood by the leaders, figuring the team could squeeze past us. The other team came at us full tilt with the musher yelling his command to pass on by. When they got within 20 feet from me, his lead dog's eyes opened wide as a deer in the headlights and skidded to a stop, wheeled around, and took off in the opposite direction. Needless to say, the musher was there for quite a while cussing and complaining before he got his dogs untangled and finally disappeared with his team in the direction from which they came.

Launching my Arctic expeditions from Two Rivers sure wasn't as easy as it was when I lived in Wiseman, Coldfoot, or the camp. Getting up there each season involved a lot more logistics and expense, so I decided to invite clients to join the trips to help defray some of the costs. My plan was to begin each season conducting a solo expedition for six weeks during the cruelest part of winter prior to taking on clients, and every other year I reserved the entire winter for me and the dogs to go strictly solo.

Hauling the dogs up to the Arctic at the beginning of every season was hectic to say the least. Most mushers' trucks are equipped with two story dog boxes that slide nicely into the bed of the truck. They can fit a whole team comfortably in individual cubbies. That might work well for 45 lb racing dogs, but dog boxes make no sense for a team of 25 burly malamutes. Not only would it require a five story box, but I'd also have to lift dogs in excess of 100 lbs up over my head to get them in. That's just unreasonable. So, instead I tethered 11 dogs in the back of the truck, and 11 in the trailer and off we went up

A quick stop at Coldfoot on our way to Deadhorse.

the Dalton Highway looking like some insane combination of the Beverly Hillbillies and a clown car with the dogs drooling on each other and their bushy tails waving in the breeze. We attracted plenty of attention from the truck drivers, and my CB radio chattered non-stop with comments about our rig.

Taking on clients again was interesting and I had the pleasure of meeting some great people and sharing the Arctic with them, but Mother Nature always seemed to reserve some of her worst weather for their trips. Two unsuspecting clients, Mark and Rae, fell victim to one of her springtime temper tantrums.

Mark, a geotechnical engineer, and Rae, a tour operator, were a couple from Anchorage, Alaska who wanted to spend 12 days with me and the team to experience the Arctic. Their first day was fantastic. Mother Nature was behaving herself and gave us warm sunshine, blue skies, and the sweet smell of willows budding in a gentle southern breeze. That afternoon we set up our tents amongst a few willows in a small, winding valley. The snow was good for cutting blocks in case there was a blizzard, but I assured Mark and Rae there was no need because we were on good terms with Mother Nature and surely she wouldn't betray us and bust our chops with a blizzard. A few hours after I made that promise, we were cutting snow blocks and preparing for a blizzard.

Being in an arctic blizzard feels like standing at the outlet end of a snow blower. And it's vital that this snow blower effect is deflected away from the tent door to prevent snow from coming inside when the door is unzipped and opened. With a simple carpenter's hand saw, snow blocks can be cut in about 2x2 foot chunks then stacked like bricks on the windward side of the tent.

As the wind gained velocity, Mark and Rae proudly brought to my attention their eloquent snow block wall that was perfectly constructed, obviously designed with an engineer's perspective. Satisfied with their work, they called it a night and crawled into their comfortable abode.

Late that night, I woke up from the sounds of blowing snow hitting the canvas wall of my tent. I knew right then, the real blizzard had come. The wind sounded like jets flying overhead and waves of snow were burying our little fortress. I quickly put on my mukluks and parka then crawled out the door to check on the dogs and secure gear that wanted a free flight to Siberia in the 70 mph wind. I cut a few snow blocks and stacked them in front of the older dogs to block the wind. They've endured their share of blizzards and they really appreciate having a little extra coverage from the blasting wind and snow.

Early the following morning I awoke to the sound of silence. Either the wind stopped or the tent was entombed in snow. I crawled out of my sleeping bag, reached across the floor and pushed on the tent door. Sure enough, I unzipped the door,

Mark and Rae's tent buried after a hurricane-force windstorm. (photo by Rae Woodsum)

exposing a solid wall of hard packed snow.

I took the snow shovel that I kept in my tent and jabbed the wall of snow until it broke free near the top of the door then I squeezed out of the opening. The skies were bright blue, and the air was still. The sleds were completely buried and the dogs were curled up sleeping. I scanned the landscape toward Mark and Rae's tent. There was nothing, just a flat white horizon of snow and a lonely stovepipe sticking straight up out of the ground reflecting the morning sun light. It looked both tranquil and triumphant kind of like a memorial after a battle. There was no smoke streaming out of it. I walked over and stood above the stove pipe, held my breath and listened for signs of life. Then there was a faint and very polite plea for help beneath the snow.

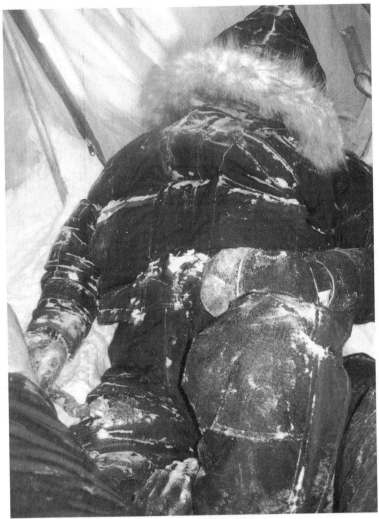

Mark inside the tent. (photo by Rae Woodsum)

I am sure Mark and Rae felt desperate in their situation, but I was chuckling so hard while digging them out I could hardly hold on to the shovel. After all, I had found myself in the same predicament quite a few times.

Mark and Rae were unharmed by the experience. They admitted they were comfortably warm in their tent, and had no idea it was buried under six feet of hard packed snow until they unzipped the door. They couldn't believe the wall of solid white staring back at them.

Mark and Rae had a cheerful and resilient attitude about their entire experience, but I have to admit I was surprised when a few years later they announced their engagement and asked if I could perform the ceremony out in the woods with the dogs and set up a camp for them. I was honored that they chose to celebrate their special day that way and I knew they'd have a happy and successful marriage. If they could endure being trapped together under six feet of snow they could deal with any of the hardships life threw at them.

So, one early December afternoon under winter's setting sun, Mark and Rae became husband and wife on the banks of a beautiful Interior Alaska river.

CHAPTER 8

The Wild Side

After many years conducting Arctic expeditions I've had a good share of encounters with wildlife. I hold all of God's creatures with the highest respect, but I recognize that some predatory animals will kill a person or a dog to satisfy their hunger. Some of the less fierce critters, although they don't intend any harm, can sure stir up trouble.

***

One of my wildlife encounters was with a grizzly bear during the Project Leffingwell Expedition. I had spent the first few weeks of the expedition caching supplies in various locations for later use. One day, while returning to pick up one of the caches we were hit mid-day with a blizzard, so I stopped the team and set up camp. After the dogs were staked out and fed I settled into my tent and listened to the snow beat against the canvas like a sand blaster until it was completely buried.

The following morning it was calm, but the temperature plummeted down to -50°F. As I prepared to hit the trail I loaded the last few (and probably most important) items on top of the sled—a double bit axe for checking ice thickness and my rifle. Normally at extreme sub zero temperatures I would pull

Out with the team dropping a cache. (photo by Germán A. Obando)

the bolt out of the rifle and put it in my pocket so it would stay warm and ready for action. If I didn't, the firing pin would most likely freeze and the chance of the rifle firing reliably would be slim. But, since I was far from the Arctic coast I didn't feel threatened by polar bears and grizzly bears were still in hibernation, so I didn't bother pulling out the bolt.

When I began hitching up the team I started to get that feeling—that subtle intuition that something wasn't quite right. I felt uneasy putting Farmer, a slower paced dog, in lead next to Bear and Boss. So I replaced Farmer with Little Savage, another fast leader.

The dogs were crazy with anticipation to get going, and they howled continuously until I gave them the command to go. Little Savage seemed overjoyed at being selected as one of the elites that day and kicked it into high gear, energizing the whole team.

Helping the dogs pull the sleds. (photo by Germán A. Obando)

The sun beat down on us as we made our way across the snow-covered tundra. Through my fogged up sunglasses I spotted a dark object above us on a cliff. I took my sunglasses off to get a better look and was shocked at what I saw—a grizzly bear charging right for us! No doubt it was a starving, killer bear out of his den in the dead of winter hunting for meat, any kind of meat. My heart felt like it was going to explode as the adrenaline shot through me. I had to get the dogs running in the opposite direction and get out of there as quickly as possible. I jumped off the runners and sprinted to the front of the team. I grabbed the leaders and swung them around 180 degrees, and gave the command to go. As the team took off I gripped the handlebars and jumped on the runners as the sled went by. I shouted out the command to make the dogs run faster and the leaders instantly responded, accelerating to a fast lope.

I started unlashing my rifle, but at the same time I was visualizing defending the dogs with my axe. I knew dang well my rifle was frozen and most likely it wouldn't fire. I also knew that if that rifle didn't shoot I was in a battle that I probably would never win. I noticed the bear's dark brown hackles over his shoulders standing up in attack mode. His massive chest muscles vibrated in rhythm with every gallop. Thick steam rolled out of his nostrils as he gained momentum. I could see the indentations of his ribs under his fur and it was clear he was starving. He was desperate and this was his last attempt to survive the throes of winter before Mother Nature drew her sword and ended him. But we had to survive, too. The bear and I locked eyes—time had run out.

Click—the rifle didn't fire. A rush of cold sweat started pouring down my face. I shoved in another cartridge, pulled the trigger and another muted click came from the firing pin. I tossed the rifle on the sled and grabbed my axe, disheartened that the scenario I had envisioned was becoming a reality, and brought it up to my shoulder. Then I commanded the dogs to stop, stepped off the runners and stood poised to meet the mad, charging grizzly bear. Deep down I knew I didn't stand a chance of killing him with an axe, but I wasn't going to let him slaughter my dogs without a fight. That bear was going to have to go through me first. After whispering a short prayer, I flung a few choice words at the bear and prepared for the battle. He stopped like he hit a fence and stood up on his two hind legs, pulled his massive paws in toward himself and stared at us. That was the most intense two seconds of my life, but I didn't stick around to see what would happen next.

As we sped away, I looked back at the bear. He looked like a giant, the king of the Arctic, watching his prey quickly slip away. It was all over and everything fell silent except the sound of my pounding heart.

Hightailing it away from the bear.

***

The dogs and I have had many experiences with wolves over the years, some more pleasant than others. My most bitter memories of wolves are the times they had claimed the lives of my dogs. However, not all of my encounters with wolves ended in tragedy and there have been many times that I've been intrigued and entertained by their intelligent and cunning nature.

While breaking trail on an expedition I caught a glimpse of a large wolf weaving between the willows alongside the river. He didn't resemble a typical arctic wolf at all. His shoulders were too broad and thick, and his coat was a brownish-red color that mimicked the hue of tundra grass in autumn. But he had those tell-tale eyes, those classic, hungry, yellow-green wolf eyes.

I had seen his tracks the day before as I dipped my coffee pot into the clear water where steam spiraled up from a thermal spring. The tracks on the river bank reminded me of a wolf that had stalked me and the team several years before. His tracks sank deep into the snow, just like these tracks did. He'd had a brownish-red coat, too. He was stout with a deep chest and muscular shoulders that supported a large square head, like a malamutes head, not like a lean arctic wolf's head.

As the team and I traveled, ptarmigan flushed in the giant wolf's wake as he lingered beside the river, making himself virtually invisible in the thick willow brush. Farmer, one of my lead dogs, glanced nervously toward the giant wolf (whom I will refer to as G.W.) who was hiding in the willows. Running next to Farmer were my two other lead dogs, Bear and Boss, who didn't care for the smell of that wolf either.

That evening I set up my canvas tent on a small hill overlooking the river and tied the dogs out on a picket line that stretched toward the river. I was concerned for Farmer and the other guys who were tethered to the line farthest away from my tent. They wouldn't stand a chance if G.W. struck in the night. I grabbed my old WWII .303 British rifle, the stock of which was smooth from wear, and prepared it for the evening. It's a fine rifle that is reliable in extremely cold weather and it has saved my life and the dogs' quite a few times from charging grizzly bears and wolves that attacked the dogs. I checked the chamber and clip to make sure they were fully loaded with 10 cartridges, picked up my binoculars off the sled and searched down river for G.W.

My eyes led me to some large tracks that followed beside the sled trail, zigzagged across the river, and disappeared into the thick willows. I knew G.W. would follow us, and sure enough, he had. He was getting hungry and the dogs were an easy target on the picket line.

I glassed up the valley where the river split and braided

Farmer, Bear, and Boss pulling with passion. (photo by Angus Mill)

through the willows whose branches were spotted white with roosting ptarmigan. Further upriver, a jagged canyon forced all the meanders of the river back together. Just above the canyon, sitting atop a windswept grassy knoll was G.W. I focused my binoculars on his head as he laid his ears back, slowly lifting his muzzle toward the darkening skies, and let out a low howl that crept down the river, carried by the wind. The malamutes raised their heads toward the heavens and eased into a low unsettling howl. G.W.'s voice became stronger in a mournful song, and then rose in pitch. As G.W. grabbed his second breath, the entire team joined in, and united in a tune that echoed throughout the valley.

Just as swiftly as the howling started, it stopped. The dogs turned their heads upriver towards G.W.'s last whimpering call, then laid down and curled up, covering their muzzles with their tails, and closed their eyes.

Howling with the wolves.

G.W. and I watched each other until dark. I knew he wouldn't sleep. I was sure he had planned to wait patiently and learn our routine so he could try to catch us off guard. Then he would slip into camp at night, killing the smallest and the most vulnerable dog, tearing him off the picket line and dragging him away. By the time I came to the rescue with my rifle, it would all be over, just like it had happened before.

I moved the smaller dogs close to my tent. I figured G.W. wouldn't come close to the tent, but still I worried for the other guys. They were bigger and stronger, but they would still be no match for G.W. It was a gut wrenching situation and it seemed like there was no way I could win, no matter how I rearranged the dogs on the picket line. If a wolf can take down a half ton moose, a dog wouldn't be a problem. Besides, after living amongst wolves for 30 years and knowing their cunning nature, I knew that old G.W. would come in that night and attack , no doubt about it. I just had that intuition. I had to think of something to spoil G.W's devilish scheme.

The only thing that came to mind was a tactic I had learned as a kid growing up in Michigan. A bunch of crows kept getting into our corn fields and pilfering our crop. My dad tried all kinds of things to keep them out of the corn, but the only thing that worked was the old scarecrow he constructed by stuffing my old, worn out clothes with straw. Dad then drove an old wooden fence pole into the soft soil next to the corn, and stood the headless dummy up against it. He placed an old soccer ball on top of its shoulders, grabbed my old baseball cap, set it on top of the soccer ball, and leaned a stick against the scarecrow's arms to resemble a gun. Dad stepped back, admired his work, adjusted the scare crow's arms, and walked back up the steps and into the house. In the dim evening light, the scarecrow looked just like a person standing there. The crows circled over the scarecrow, cackled, cried, and flew away towards our neighbors' corn field.

Why not give it a try, I thought. If it worked on a crow maybe it would work on that hungry wolf. So, I built my own scarecrow by the farthest dog on the picket line, Farmer. I stuck two skis in the snow side by side, draped my parka over them, propped the sleeves up with ski poles and stuffed a stocking cap into the parka hood. Holy smokes, it looked like a real person as the ice fog settled around it.

After a few adjustments to the ski poles I went inside my tent and waited and listened. The noises outside the tent sounded magnified in my nervous anticipation. I held my breath, thinking I heard footsteps in the snow as the dogs shuffled around and shook the frost off their coats. My heart pounded when a ptarmigan flushed out of the willows down by the river. Even the scampering of a mouse dashing across the tent floor caused me to imagine G.W. was right outside my tent door. I felt assured though, with my rifle beside me. I reached over and grabbed the gun several times during the night, rehearsing the scene and knowing exactly what I'd do if G.W. decided to slither into camp. Memories of the dogs I'd lost to wolves in the past tormented me all night—the pup's collar lying on the snow, torn in two, and a trail of blood leading away. I sat up all night on my sleeping bag, wearing my mukluks and parka with my rifle resting across my lap, and waited until the stars succumbed to the morning light.

As the glow of the sun rose I was ready to get outside my tent and shake the chill out of my stiff, tired muscles. The scarecrow looked eerie in the gray light with ice fog lingering above it, almost like a man standing in a cloud. I trotted down to the river, counting dogs as I went by them. Not more than 15 yards from Farmer were a set of large wolf tracks. They came from upriver in a perfectly straight line, like G.W. was on a very calculated mission. His stride became shorter as he approached Farmer. But he stopped short of his target, turned away, and ran down river, wavering back and forth as if he was watching his backside.

He had come awfully close, so I knew G.W. would not scare away easily. His stomach had to be nagging the heck out of him. He needed meat to survive and he definitely has his eyes on the dogs. If G.W. did not find something to eat soon, he would die and be another wolf's meal.

Farmer was anxious to get going that morning. I figured he must have had an unsettling smell of G.W. that night. I quickly fed the dogs, broke camp and hitched up the team. We traveled upriver, entering a twisted, rocky canyon filled with thigh-deep snow. The canyon widened into a broad valley and rugged mountains towered powerfully above us with jagged peaks ascending toward the red February sun.

After the dogs and I had a fine day of mushing, I had worked up quite an appetite and looked forward to some fried ptarmigan, a hot cup of coffee, and a crackling fire in my wood burning stove. Yet, G.W. was tugging on my mind. As I stuck my tent poles in the snow, G.W. began to howl. His song was very faint and sounded as though he was high above the camp on the mountain side.

I thought maybe G.W. was howling out of loneliness as I suspected was the case with a lone female wolf I'd seen in the Arctic many years prior. The northern lights were brilliant orange, purple and hazy green that night and as she howled, the team joined in with her melodious song intermittently, but they were weary from the day's hard work and eventually fell silent and slept. But she kept howling. I guessed she was waiting for an answer from her lifelong mate. Maybe he had been killed, fallen off a cliff hunting sheep or fatally kicked by a moose. Ever since, I've wondered what ever became of her. Did she find another mate? Did another wolf pack find her, and, if so, did they let her live or did an alpha female destroy her?

G.W. continued to howl throughout the evening. His hymns seemed to blend in with the landscape, like the darkening jagged mountains, and the white, treeless tundra. Suddenly, I heard another voice, an unfamiliar and higher pitched howl that came from across the river. My heart sank. Now two wolves would be on the prowl tonight.

I tried to stay awake all night, but I just couldn't keep my eyes open. I was exhausted and I couldn't fight sleep any longer, no matter how much I wanted to stay alert to the threat of the wolves. As I dozed off that night in my tent I dreamed about the problems I'd had with wolves in the past. I dreamed about one terrible night when the snow was blowing sideways across the tundra as I searched frantically with my headlight for a sign, any kind of sign, of those green, glowing wolf eyes. There they flashed, behind the brush. I raised my rifle, aiming for the wolf, but second guessed myself. *What if it's my pup and he's still alive,* I thought, and then lowered the rifle, deciding not to shoot in the dark. If only I had stayed awake that night. Would the pup still be with me today?

I awoke early the next morning to the sounds of ptarmigan wings gliding over the top of my tent. I quickly rushed outside, relieved to see the dogs were nestled in their beds, sleeping comfortably. I ran past them to the river and came across G.W.'s tracks. Just like the day before, the tracks trailed from upriver. But, this time, a smaller set of tracks came from the opposite direction and met G.W.'s trail, intermixing with his large prints. Some of the paw prints were washed out with small pools of yellow urine and some were scratched through the snow, leaving claw marks on the ice. Other prints showed that the two wolves stood nose to nose, but there was no blood from a fight. The two sets of tracks then trailed off together, single file, small tracks atop G.W.'s tracks, and disappeared in the willows.

I never saw G.W. again that winter. I suspect his attention shifted to his new mate and they found food together somehow. Maybe he's still out there teaching hunting skills to his new offspring. I will never know for sure.

***

Of course, not all wildlife in the Arctic is dangerous. Some critters are a nuisance more than anything. We were camped in narrow river valley and Little Savage was having the time of her life, running free and catching voles—those fury little mouse-like rodents that scurry around in the tundra grass. I wasn't nearly as enthused about the voles as Savage. The black arctic voles were everywhere. I couldn't take another minute of it, and I didn't care about the blizzard coming. I just wanted to get away from them. They were crawling in my sleeping bag, scampering across my dinner plate, and getting tangled up in

Little Savage gets harassed by Red.

my hair at night. Heck, they even took up living quarters inside my beaver fur mitts.

I hated to leave that camp site, especially with that dark blizzard creeping over the hill. From the size of it, it didn't look friendly. I knew I had better stay put and not risk traveling. But, I wasn't going to bed down with those beady, black-eyed varmints again. No... not for another night. I was getting out of there, come hell or high water.

As peeved as I was about the voles, I got a good chuckle watching Little Savage, my 3-month old pup, chasing those buggers around camp. She would sprint after them, pounce like a fox, clumsily missing her target, then run back to me, scared, as the panicked vole ran in circles searching for something to hide under.

Voles aside, it was a wonderful place to camp, the kind of place that's just begging to be explored, and it was great spot for hunting. There were plenty of dry willows for firewood alongside the frozen river and lots of ptarmigan roosting in the brush nearby. The snow was only above my ankles and there were fresh caribou tracks on the hill above camp. From the hill, looking south, you could see the narrow river valley that weaved between the hill and a high mountain. Lying directly in the path of the strong west wind, the mountain's gentle slope lay exposed, with tall brown grass and small, intermittent patches of snow. Cut deep into the grass and snow, just below the rock strewn mountain peak was a dall sheep trail that wandered south. Further up the valley there was a towering canyon, jagged and gray, like a giant stone gate.

The team and I followed the river through that canyon two days earlier, before the vole attack. It was colder then, about -30°F, and the sun's golden rays had finally pierced over the horizon after being absent for a long two months. It was pleasant, and it didn't feel cold anymore when the sun broke the shadows in the canyon and settled on the dogs and me. I felt the dogs speed up as the light hit them. They were as glad as I was to see the sun again.

Just past the canyon, the river led us to a small lake surrounded by low hills. The lake, shaped like a half moon with a few struggling willows drooping over its banks, didn't look like much as far as fishing goes, but I thought I'd give it a try anyway. After about 30 minutes of chipping away with my chisel, I broke through four feet of ice. Crystal clear water gushed and gurgled up to the top of the hole and seeped around its edges.

I tied some heavy thread to a willow stick, pulled off about 60 feet from the spool, tied a hook to the end of it, baited it with a sliver of fresh ptarmigan meat and a small white feather, and plopped it down the hole. The hook and bait sank slowly, and then rested on the lake's bottom. I wound the remaining string around the stick and raised the bait up a few inches off the bottom and jigged it. Almost right away I felt a strike, nearly pulling the stick out of my hand. I pulled back. It felt solid, like I had hooked a rock. Then I felt the vibration, the kind of powerful thrashing you feel from a large fish's desperate struggle when he's first hooked. Since I didn't have much line to let him run on, I just held the stick tight with both hands, hoping he wouldn't snap the line or tear the hook from his mouth. He tired quickly though, and I worked him slowly up, pulling the string hand over hand with the icy water freezing to my mitts. Before the fish's snout was even visible in the hole I envisioned him sizzling in my skillet and Little Savage crunching on her favorite fish head meal. I eased him up out of the water and tossed him, flailing, on the ice. Little Savage jumped off the sled and ran over pawing and sniffing the 10 lb lake trout.

But the fun was over and I had to leave this place.

"Yes, Little Savage, it was a fine camp," I mumbled as she watched me toss my sleeping bag in the sled.

"Too bad girl, maybe we'll be back when it cools off."

She glared at me with those dark puppy eyes, cocked her head sideways, and turned away. Just then, she swiped a glance at a mouse dashing out of the tent, and pounced on it. "Good girl," I praised her.

The blizzard was coming on fast. Dark clouds rolled over the hill toward us. Strangely though, there was a springtime smell in the wind, the kind of fresh, green willow bud aroma that you can almost taste while you walk on the tundra during summer solstice as the wildflowers bloom. Clearly it wasn't summer, and the winter solstice had just passed, but it did feel warm, 45°F, I guessed. The snow had melted a little on the river bank where the ptarmigan were nibbling on those tiny, white quartz stones, filling their gizzards with them. And the mice were crawling out of their winter nests and pillaging the tundra and tormenting its inhabitants. I knew the Chinook, wouldn't

The day's catch.

stay long. Usually it lasts a few days, and then winter returns. Every year she blows over the Brooks Range from the south, bringing warmth, deep snow and hurricane force winds with her. But those doggone voles apparently had no clue.

I quickly took down my canvas tent, folded it up, loaded the sleds and hitched up the team. Little Savage was busy chasing voles when I gave the dogs the command to go. She came running behind the sleds as the team started down the winding river with her tongue hanging out the side of her mouth.

"Good girl", I encouraged her as she caught up to me. Standing on the runners, I turned around and picked her up and set her on the sled. She settled down comfortably on the folded tent with the west wind waving her red and white coat. While she lay there, I noticed how she had grown handsomely in her first three months of life. I wondered if one day she would become a leader. She seemed to have her dad's brains, and she was a fast runner as well.

Little Savage was only 10 days old when we left the hunting camp in November. She hadn't seen another person, besides me, for her entire three months of life. She looked up to me like a child, with vulnerable and trusting eyes. Her entire life's experience had been on the arctic trail, the kind of existence that every Alaskan malamute must dream about.

Little Savage raised her head as the wind hit us with a short, powerful gust. It was just a warning shot, but I had already committed to leaving. I wished I had stayed but there was no use looking back. We had to keep moving. The freight team of 22 malamutes trotted down the widening river which linked into an east-west trending tributary that was whipped clear of snow. The team turned onto it and headed straight into the increasing wind.

I wanted to travel as far as I could that day despite the storm so I could get as far from the voles as possible and so I could find a place to set up camp where there was a good stand of willows, which are few and far between. Then I planned to take a couple days off from traveling to repair gear, clothing, and harnesses. As the team followed the river toward the low hills, the clouds that were dark before had now turned a misty light gray. Those were not the same dark clouds I saw earlier. I knew right then, those clouds equated to a wave of snow, the kind that precedes an awfully mean blizzard. The storm was moving quickly, swallowing the hills as it approached.

We were heading straight into the blizzard's heart. At first, her whipping winds knocked me around a little as I trotted next to the sled, holding onto the handle bars as I urged the team onward. Then she tossed a few waves of snow, willow leaves and some sand my way. *Nothing I can't deal with, she's just harassing me*, I told myself. Then I heard that horrible rushing sound, very faint and far away. The sound reminded me of rustling leaves on a windy fall day when I was a kid growing up in Michigan, a pleasant sound, but I knew the very guts of it, and she was about to take off her disguise and turn into an ugly, tearing force. The gust came closer. Soon, you could hear it like a jet coming in for a landing.

I yelled toward the leaders to stop. I doubled over, braced myself against the sled, put one hand gently on Little Savage, and grabbed my fur parka hood and pulled it over my face with my other hand. The gust hit hard and pounded us with a solid wave of snow and let off. I knew it was just a preliminary gust, just an appetizer before the main course of bone chilling, whipping, eye-stinging wind and snow. I had no choice but to call it for what it was and reside to the fact she was going to whip our butts if I didn't find cover, and quick. But what cover? The river was barren of deep snow for the dogs to curl up and shield themselves, and I had to have firewood to wait out a possible nonstop, 3-day blast from one of Mother Nature's nastiest tools—the blizzard. I knew I had played a game of dead man's bluff with Mother Nature and she had the winning hand. Mother Nature is like Dr. Jekyll and Mr. Hyde—one entity, split in two, and I didn't know whom I was dealing with...the devious Hyde, or Jekyll. Either she'd allow the wind to subside so we could continue or she'd unleash hell on us and pound us without relief. I started to figure it was the latter.

Soon, she opened the wind's gate. The wall of snow hit us, and I lost my footing at first. I held tightly onto the sled and reached for Little Savage. She felt fine, although she was shivering. The team continued in a struggled, slow pace. I worked my way to the leaders, stopped the team and wiped the snow off the lead dogs' eyes. They were traveling blind. I tried to search ahead for cover, but I couldn't see any farther than my hand in front of me, and the ground and sky were one fluid mass of white.

Traveling as a blizzard starts to move in. *(photo by Angus Mill)*

The wind whipped wet snow mercilessly on us. I turned my back to the wind's onslaught and leaned back to keep my balance. Mother Nature had us beat. She called my bluff and showed her cards. She caught me foolishly in the open and would pound and splinter me for my hasty mistake. We advanced through the war zone, working off the river and searching the tundra for a decent place to camp. I just didn't have the heart to give up. My shoulders whipped back with her gusts like someone shoved me and my stride was reduced to nothing more than baby steps.

The land was grayish white and getting darker by the minute as I struggled to lead the dogs. I felt the contour of the tussocks and the soft, shallow snow under my caribou hide mukluks as I walked. I heard small sticks tumble past my feet, and then a large, dry willow stick ricocheted off my shin. It was time to admit Mother Nature had me beat and figure out a way to make camp on the miserable, bare tundra.

I decided to search ahead of the team a few more yards before calling it quits. A dark object emerged. A winter grizzly bear! Or so I thought. It wasn't moving and I realized it was a dwarfed willow. As I stepped closer to it my foot sank into knee deep snow. I worked back to the leaders and urged them to follow until the entire team was in the willows. The dogs immediately began digging into the protection of the deep snow while I set Little Savage off the sled and pulled out my tent and poles. Fumbling, I stuck the aluminum tent poles into the snow, right next to the sled, forming the tent frame. Then I yanked the snapping, flapping, beating-like-a-giant-goose-wing canvas tent over the tent frame. I tried to anyway. It was a tug-of-war. Back and forth we fought, the wind and I. She grabbed hold of it with such a jolt I thought surely I'd lose my grip on the canvas, but I held on with my life. I envisioned the tent betraying me and flying off with the wind, then I would be in for a rather painful evening, and I probably wouldn't live to tell about it.

I managed to get one side of the tent over the poles, loaded several bags of dog food on the edge of the canvas and pinned down the opposite side with more dog food bags, then quickly shoveled snow over the entire outside perimeter of the tent.

The snow had covered the dogs, so they were safe and comfortable, but Little Savage whined. I grabbed my sleeping bag and floor tarp and tucked her up under my arm and crawled into the tent. I set her down and unrolled my sleeping bag. Little Savage jumped excitedly to her feet, pounced on the sleeping bag and pulled out a squirming, black, buggy-eyed vole clinched between her canines. She sat wagging her tail, showing off her prize.

"Good girl, Little Savage. Good girl," I chuckled.

CHAPTER 9

Minds of Their Own

The things that make every dog sledding expedition memorable aren't always wildlife encounters, panoramic scenery, or the exhilaration of exploring. It's the dogs. I love watching the dogs' interaction with one another, and to see them grow from puppies into adulthood. I have been blessed with so many outstanding dogs over the years.

Bear was insanely intelligent and ridiculously stubborn for a dog, but the characteristic that really stood out in him was his unwavering courage. Nothing bothered him. It seemed he was invincible. He led us many times straight into 60 mph wind gusts, blinding blizzards, and over steep mountain passes without ever second guessing his confidence. He had an all-or-nothing, get the job done come hell or high water attitude.

When Bear was a pup I knew right away he would become a leader. He was friendly, loved interaction with people, and was very athletic. As he grew into adolescence he didn't show any interest in the team's hierarchy, which is another trait of a great leader.

During his first run in the team at two years of age, Bear spent most of the time observing the terrain rather than pulling. He was mesmerized by the landscape and its elements, taking it all in, analyzing and processing it.

Bear, Boss, and Farmer in lead. (photo by Angus Mill)

After a while Bear started pulling with true, malamute passion. Nothing could slow him down or disturb his labor of love. At three years old, I placed him in lead beside his father, Teddy. When we began training for the Project Leffingwell Expedition, Bear's true character revealed itself.

I was preparing to take the dogs on an overnight training run. It was November and the temperature was around -20°F and windy. There was about six inches of fresh snow on the trail as I hitched a team of dogs to a sled loaded with my tent and gear. The trail wound up the river valley and then over a low pass by a craggy mountainside where we had camped a week earlier. Teddy and Bear ran side by side, leading the team. Once in a while, I noticed Bear glance at the mountain. I figured he saw caribou in that direction and I didn't pay a lot of attention to his strange behavior. Then, Bear jerked Teddy off the trail, turned the team toward the mountain and leaned into

116

Heading into the mountains.

his harness for all he was worth. I was curious to see what Bear was up to, so I let him break trail where he wanted to go.

Bear seemed obsessed with that mountain, and corrected his route every time we had to circumvent an obstacle like thick brush. Eventually, I realized Bear was heading straight for our old campsite and apparently he didn't want to waste time following a trail. He was taking a shortcut and using the mountain peak 12 miles away like a compass.

Before we had left, Bear watched me load the tent and dog food in the sled. He knew exactly where I had planned to go and had it all figured out. In his brain, he had our trip planned for us.

From that point on, Bear began to exhibit strong leadership and focus. In fact, he became so absorbed in his work that he was oblivious to things that happened around him.

Once, we were traveling through a deep canyon that cut between two tall and jagged mountains with heavy, deep snow on their slopes. The wind was howling between the canyon walls directly into our faces. It wasn't too cold, but visibility was about 50 feet. Bear and Teddy were in lead and I trudged behind the sled, holding onto the handlebars with one hand, and pulling my hood down with the other, protecting my face from the stinging snow.

Suddenly, I felt a shudder under my feet. I jumped on the sled runners and told Bear and Teddy to *hit*. The team lunged into their harnesses, but it was too late. The avalanche barreled down the slope, pushing sticks and willow brush ahead of it, followed by an ocean wave of snow. The dogs tried to jump and scramble away, instead they got tangled in the lines and created a big knot, but Bear stayed calm and focused and plodded straight forward.

The avalanche, slammed on the river, leveled off to about two feet high and pushed against the sleds and the dogs and stopped us in our tracks, yet it didn't concern Bear he kept trying to pull. He had a job to do and by golly, he was going to get it done!

Everyone in the team came to respect Bear. He was a strong leader in every aspect. The dogs sensed his strength and wisdom. Through blizzards, across thin ice, or through deep snow the team stayed in perfect step with him and followed him faithfully. When Bear turned one way or another, the team swung graciously with him. As he struggled up a mountain pass, the other dogs dug in and pulled in earnest, and when we got on sea ice and Bear stretched out in a lope, everyone followed him enthusiastically.

On Christmas day, we were camped at the base of a mountain pass and had been pounded by a blizzard that entire day and night. When the storm subsided, I noticed that the high winds had blown the snowpack off the mountain pass,

The team pulling three sleds tied in tandem into the Brooks Range.
(photo by Germán A. Obando)

exposing bare gravel. The sleds were heavily loaded with three months of supplies and I knew the dogs wouldn't be able to pull the entire load over the gravely summit. I decided to cache most of the supplies at the campsite and retrieve it after snow conditions improved. I hitched the team with Bear in lead and we reached the summit in six hours against a light northern wind that bit our faces. I set up camp on the pass, fed the team and watched the northern lights perform their ritual dance in an array of green and purple hues.

The next morning, the temperature was around -45°F and the skies were clear as I hitched up the team. I placed Angel, a young, energetic female next to Bear to give him extra confidence for the descent down the steep slope.

Bear slowly trotted down the pass, and skillfully chose wide curved routes around the crevasses. After a few hours we reached the valley floor and swiftly crossed the river ice and then followed a winding creek toward a distant peak that struck me as very unique. The gray limestone spire stood out above the landscape.

We followed the creek which led us onto a high plateau where there were hundreds of towering peaks as far as I could see. At the bottom of the plateau, a narrow river twisted up a valley where several caribou were feeding on the hillside. I pulled out my binoculars and focused in on them, and then I looked upriver toward a dark, narrow canyon. At the canyon's entrance was a patch of thick willows perfect for a campsite.

I set my binoculars back in its case, stood on the sled runners and gave the command to go. The team ran down the slope with their tails waving high. As the sleds came off the sloping bank, they slammed on the river ice. I slipped off the runners and went down hard on my knee. An excruciating pain shot through my leg. I shook it off, bit my tongue, stepped on the runners and continued upriver. I found a small clearing in the willows where I set up my tent and staked the dogs out on the picket line and settled in for the evening.

That night, temperatures dropped to -60°F but the valley had a pleasant atmosphere with the moonlight reflecting off the river ice in the ravine, illuminating the rocky cliffs. But the following morning I was in no mood to appreciate nature's tranquil beauty. My knee was swelled double in size, sore as heck and stiff as a board. I tried working it loose for a few hours and managed to get it to move a little, but I wasn't able to walk on it. I crawled outside the tent, dragged a bag of dog food over to the team and fed them. Then I managed to get on my feet, using my rifle case for a crutch, and limped alongside the river bank gathering firewood.

For nearly two weeks I stayed at the camp, carefully trying to nurse my knee to health. My supplies were almost gone and I knew we would have to head back to the cache. At that point, my crippled knee wasn't a consideration. I had to renew my

Into a narrow canyon.

supplies no matter how much pain I was in.

Bear and the team were well rested and anxious to get going. With light sleds, and a good trail, we made it back to the mountain pass in four days. I set up camp at the base of the pass so we could climb it with plenty of rest and energy in the morning, but the four day sled trip didn't do my knee any favors at all and it was more swollen than before.

That evening, I got a feeling that a storm was coming and I couldn't afford being pinned down in a blizzard with such a low supply of rations. The following morning, dark clouds rolled over the pass as I broke camp. I had everything tied in the sleds and was hitching up the last dog when the blizzard hit. I was teed off and I knew it would be stupid to attempt climbing the pass during a raging blizzard. That would be asking for a catastrophe. So, I unhitched everyone and set up camp again.

The wind whipped the mountain pass all day and then calmed down towards the evening. The mountain looked higher than ever before, and my knee throbbed with every heartbeat. I slept nervously that night, not because the pain in my knee was keeping me awake, but because I felt uncomfortable, like something was wrong. I tossed and turned for hours, and then finally decided to fire up the stove and have some coffee.

As I settled in to take my first sip, I heard a strong gust of wind. It was a loud blast that punched the tent like a giant fist. My coffee pot rattled on the stove and the canvas tent flapped like a wing. The gust lasted a minute and then it was silent.

I crawled across the tent, unzipped the door, and looked out across the dark, white tundra. Another southern gust brushed against my hair and the temperature felt mild. The air had a springtime smell to it.

I shined the headlamp toward the dogs. The dogs' eyes cast a green reflection off the bright light. They sat on their haunches, and looked at me curiously. Bear looked especially alert. He raised his muzzle toward the hazy green northern lights and set free a howl, an ancient tune. The entire team chimed in, and howled a chorus that the finest opera singers couldn't mimic. In the distance, a lone wolf answered their call. It started in a muted, mournful tone and then crescendoed, inspiring the entire team in another wonderful song. The duet lasted several minutes and then silence crept across the valley.

Another wind gust swept across the tundra—another warning that a blizzard was stewing. I wasn't certain when it would hit us, but I knew we had better get out of there right away.

By the time I lashed the camp in the sleds and hitched up the team, sundogs were flaring in the morning sky. In lead, I hitched Angel and Bear next to each other, though I shortened Angel's line so she was slightly behind Bear. I wanted Bear to lead us without hindrance.

After an hour of traveling up the pass, the wind slammed us head on and pushed waves of snow, covering the sleds and dogs in a blanket of white. Visibility dropped to zero. It was a perfect white-out. It was like traveling in a cloud, a white abyss, a swirling, snowy, wind tunnel. I decided to lead the team on snowshoes. The snow stung my face like bees as the dogs followed closely behind me, but I was limping badly with sharp pain piercing my knee. As the wind gusts increased to 50 mph I found myself stumbling and barely able to stand on my snowshoes. It was too late to turn around, besides we were dangerously low on supplies. No matter what, we had to reach our cache. I turned around and lowered my knees on the snow with wrenching pain and reached out and stroked both Angel and Bear. They licked the ice off my cheeks as I encouraged them.

"Now it's your turn, Bear. It's up to you. Let Angel be your confidence, but you gotta find the way up the pass," I said loudly over the wind, putting full faith in his leadership.

I limped down the line of the dogs, encouraging each of them with pets and then shuffled to the back sled where I had a short rope tied to the handlebar. I grabbed the end of the rope and yelled, "Okay!"

The team hesitated at first and then slowly began ascending the pass. There wasn't a trail and I knew there were some deep crevasses ahead. But I trusted Bear. The wind was increasing in velocity, and to make matters worse, it was getting dark. We were bucking hurricane force gusts that seemed to tear right through me. Several long hours went by and the ground started to level. We were almost on the summit. When I dragged my watch out of my pocket, I was stunned. We had been struggling for six hours.

Finally, the wind died a little as we crested the pass and I stopped the team. I quickly limped up to Bear. His face was covered with snow and ice and his eyes were completely closed. I peeled his ice mask off and his eyes opened. He seemed to smile. He had led us up that mountain pass and through the blizzard with his eyes closed.

But the worst was still ahead of us. The snow was thigh deep and I had to break trail for the team on snowshoes. After an hour, my leg went numb, and I didn't notice a bit of pain until I found our cache six hours later.

After getting the dogs out of their harnesses and feeding them, I wrestled my canvas tent out of the sled, set it up and crawled inside. With hot flames crackling in the stove, coffee was steaming in my cup, and the wind howling outside I rested on my sleeping mats and took a moment to reflect on our struggle. The blizzard lasted six solid days and nights. Bear led the team and Angel helped him when he stumbled. Maybe when I struggled and stumbled, an angel was at my side giving me the nudge I need to continue, too.

***

Bear continued to be a great lead dog and we had a mutual respect for each other. I trusted his instincts and followed him without question, and when I led the team breaking trail, he followed me with loyalty.

On one expedition, as the dark days of January grew near, the snow became deep and snowshoeing in front of the team was the only way to make notable progress. After a long day of traveling, I made camp beside a river amongst some dry willows. Next to the willows on a windblown gravel bar flowed a warm spring. The clear spring water ran onto the river ice, through an opening, and into the river under the three foot thick ice. It was a perfect camping spot, so I decided to spend a couple days there to catch up on sled and harness repairs. Then I intended to cross the mile wide river at a point where a creek ran through the black shale bluffs on the opposite bank. The creek supplied a passage up a tight twisted canyon, then over a mountain pass.

The temperature was a comfortable -20°F with a light southwest wind and clear skies. The first night I slept comfortably and caught up on some much needed rest but on the second night I awoke in a sweat. Crawling out of my sleeping bag, I slipped on my caribou fur mukluks and rushed out to the thermometer I'd left on the sled. It read 42°F. A Chinook moving in quickly means trouble in the Arctic, and I was concerned about the condition of the ice, but the faint glow of moonlight reflected off the wind polished ice on the river, giving me ample light to see that the ice was firm and there was no water on the river—yet.

Returning to the camp, I boiled up some coffee and fried a good portion of caribou meat, knowing it would be a long day. I thawed some frozen blueberries and topped off my breakfast with raw whale blubber. I tossed each dog a healthy chunk of muktuk as well. Immediately after breakfast I heard the unmistakable sounds of ice cracking like gunshots in the distance, growing louder by the minute.

I quickly broke camp and hooked up the team. I grabbed a handful of chains out of the sled bag and hurriedly wrapped and fastened them around the sled runners to prevent the sleds from swinging side to side as we crossed the slippery ice.

By the time I fastened the chains to the runners, the dogs were excited to go. They howled impatiently, listening for the command to go. But that day I decided to lead the team myself, feeling uneasy about the cracking ice. I pulled the snow hook and told the team to stay. Then I tied the hook securely to the top of the sled with a rope to keep it from accidently falling off and hooking into the ice. Bear and Angel were in lead, watching my every move. Bear was shivering with excitement and anticipation to go. I walked past the leaders and started off

Leading the team. (photo by Angus Mill)

in a jog, telling them to come.

As I trotted across the river I could hear the dogs panting and the chains on the runners grinding on the ice behind me. As we approached the opposite side of the river my heart sank. *Too late*, I thought. Water was running and gushing against the rocky shale cliffs in a torrent. Making a quick turn upriver to avoid the water, I jogged back to the sled and grabbed my binoculars. Glancing upriver, I spotted a narrow crossing where the water didn't look as deep. I took the chains off the runners in case we broke through the ice, in which case the chains would hang up on the broken ice and cause serious problems. Water was soon flowing around us on all sides, so we had to cross where we could.

Once again trotting in front of Bear and Angel, I led them to the narrow channel of water flowing on top of the ice which was about 100 feet wide. I didn't know how deep it was, but we were committed. That first step into the cold water really got my blood moving and I ran all out to the other side. As my feet and shins became numb, I looked back at my devoted and loyal leaders. The poor dogs were practically swimming, but the leaders had the whole team following my every step just like a line of ducklings following their mama.

After reaching dry land I shed my wet mukluks and clothes, put on dry ones and gave the dogs a chance to roll in the snow and dry off and then we headed for high ground.

***

One of the many memorable experiences I've had with lead dogs is with a handsome red, thick-furred malamute named Farmer, who actually started out as a wheel dog. With a name like Farmer, you might think that he would be just a regular, run of the mill, good ol' wheel dog—someone who just minded his own business, put his nose to the grindstone and pulled all day, and howled all night. Nope, not Farmer. He had greater ambitions. He was like a guy who's built like an NFL lineman but wants to be a ballet dancer, or the man that couldn't carry a tune to save his life, but wants to sing opera.

Early on, when he was pulling in wheel, I detected his desire to pull incredibly hard, and while wearing a smile, too. Although most wheelers enjoy a good solid pull, Farmer pulled harder than the others, almost fanatically. Yet, I was reluctant to put him in lead position. He just didn't resemble a lean, agile, athletic leader. He didn't strike me as someone who could stay ahead of the team, maneuver over jumbled sea ice, or easily weave through brush. His 120 lb square-shouldered frame seemed clumsy. But his strong spirit was a true leader's trait.

Farmer, the team and I were camped at a place that I refer to as "the hell hole." This area alongside a high, gray and jagged

One of my lead dogs, Farmer. (photo by Angus Mill)

bluff had an incredible tendency for high winds. I remember one wind storm when we were pinned down in a 60 mph blow with a -90°F wind chill, I called my wife, Andrea, on the satellite phone.

"Hi, honey. Does NOAA weather have an estimate of when this wind storm will stop? It's been blowing for two solid days now," I griped.

"What windstorm? I just checked the NOAA website and it says you have clear skies and 20 mph winds up there," Andrea informed me.

And that's the way it was most of the time. It was a true hell hole trapped in its own secret environment. But, the windswept tundra was hard packed for good traveling. And the river was wide and smooth, allowing my 22-dog freight team to pull a healthy load. Musk oxen thrived there as well, grazing on the brown grasses exposed along windblown river banks. They looked like a herd of buffalo in the distance, and sometimes they wandered so close to my tent that I could hear them chew on the moss and grass. The dogs seemed to get used to them after a while, although Farmer whined like a baby when he saw those burly, long-haired beasts wander by.

As I was hitching up the team in the hell hole, a cool 30 mph breeze was freezing my fingers and turning my cheeks to ice. Farmer sat with his tail sweeping the snow, glaring at me intently.

"Okay, Farmer, you win. I'll put you in lead next to Boss and Bear, but you'd better follow what they do!" I swear just then, Farmer smiled.

Lead dog in a large Alaskan malamute team is an important position, and is normally reserved for the superbly talented elites of the team. Not just any ol' dog can run lead, but Farmer didn't believe he was just any ol' dog. In his young canine brain he was the leader, the super dog, the invincible hero that would guide his comrades through freezing cold blizzards, darkness, and across thin cracking ice. Farmer didn't know his limits. He wasn't aware that limits even existed.

Seriously though, a big team of malamutes packs a lot of power and trying to stop a runaway team with just a sled brake would be like throwing cotton balls to stop a charging bear. So that's where a good lead dog comes in. When you say stop, they stop. When you tell them to go, the entire team hits their harnesses, and if the leaders are out of control, frankly, the team is out of control, regardless of how many cuss words you throw at them.

Anyhow, I thought the hell hole would be a fine area for Farmer to start training for lead. The tundra was wide open and he couldn't get us in trouble—or so I thought. Farmer stepped into his harness. I slipped the neck piece over his head, hooked my finger under his collar and placed him between Boss and

Bear in lead. Farmer immediately slobbered on Boss's neck and growled at Bear.

"Alright, Farmer! You behave or you'll be pulling with the wheelers again," I scolded him. He looked at me, wagged his brushy red and white tail, and straightened his huge, square shoulders. It was almost comical how he towered over Bear and Boss. Farmer tried unsuccessfully to look serious with one ear drooped over and the other ear standing up. The red bristles on his back stood up as straight as cut grass as he poised himself, ready for the command to go. He was beaming with pride.

"Okay!" I yelled loudly over the wind. Bear, Boss and Farmer hit their harnesses and the team followed. Bear directed the team on a straight course alongside the river with Boss and Farmer pulling beside him. Farmer looked majestic with his vibrant reddish-white coat and his thick tail filtering the golden sunrise. His harness straps were tight as a drum while he leaned forward and I started to wonder why I hadn't put him in lead earlier.

Just then, Farmer lowered his head, his muzzle a few inches off the snow, and started pulling with every ounce of strength he could muster. The rest of the team felt his energy and followed. The pace picked up. I hopped onto the back sled as they sped up.

Farmer turned hard right, pulling Bear and Boss reluctantly along with him.

"Haw, haw!" I yelled. It was no use. Farmer was on a mission, and he didn't give a darn about what I had to say. He was going to pull the entire team with him and there was nothing I could to do to stop him.

I held on tight as the sleds slid across glare ice, gaining speed as Farmer, still with his muzzle close to the ground, zigzagged like he was chasing the wind. The team followed his every nonsensical move and the three freight sleds fish-tailed back and forth.

Musk oxen.

Before I knew it we were cruising fast across the river and the entire team was absorbed in Farmers fanatical scheme. I didn't know whether to laugh or scream. I stood on the brake and half-heartedly commanded the team to slow down, but I knew Farmer was completely tuned out. Boss and Bear skidded a little on their butts when they heard the command, and a few of the others slacked their lines but Farmer's infectious energy had now captured the entire team.

What is cooking in Farmers brain and why was he so crazed, I thought. Then I saw the reason for Farmer's insanity—musk ox turds. They rolled, bounced, slid and flew with the wind ahead of his nose. I couldn't believe it! We were chasing musk oxen turds across the Arctic. And Farmer was determined to catch and eat those little black balls.

And, of course, where there's smoke there's fire. In the

distance, and getting closer by the second, the turd-makers had already taken position in a circle to defend themselves from the maniac dog team approaching. I bet we looked like the most ungodly sight that those musk oxen had ever seen.

As we came nearer, the big bulls squeezed tighter together, protecting the cows and calves behind them. I felt like we were a fast flying baseball headed for a solid wooden bat.

Finally I saw the opportunity coming up to stop the team and get them headed away from the musk oxen. As the sled runners glided off the river ice, they dragged on a sand bar, just enough so that I could hop off the sled and sprint ahead of Farmer and turn him around. The musk oxen were so close I could hear the bulls grunting, probably saying, *Stay behind me kids, these fools have no clue what they have coming.*

A few expedition seasons after our turd-chasing ordeal, Farmer grew into quite a lead dog, busting trails across the Arctic and living up to the old saying: *ordinary dogs have done extraordinary things because they didn't know they couldn't.*

CHAPTER 10

A Fighter's Spirit

Of all the dogs I've ever had, there was one in particular that had stolen my heart in so many ways. Her name was Boss, and her name fit her personality like a glove.

Boss was born on a beautiful spring day. The morning sun felt pleasantly warm as I opened my cabin door. Above, flocks of geese migrating north covered the bright blue sky and cackling ptarmigan echoed up the river valley as I walked over to Angel's dog house. She lay curled up tight inside with her muzzle under her bushy white tail. Raising her head, she licked my hand as I reached and felt her tight tummy. I was anxious for the puppies' arrival. It was spring in the Arctic and time for new life.

I spent the day hunting caribou, leaving Angel alone and giving her opportunity to relax. The migrating cow caribou were plump, bellies bulging and about to calve. That didn't slow them down, though. They kept wandering north over the low rolling hills to their coastal calving grounds. The bulls were herded up together following them. They grew nervous as I approached. I harvested two bulls and packed the meat back to camp.

That afternoon, delicate yellow songbirds were dashing to and fro in the budding willows beside Angel's house as I checked on her progress. She was panting and getting awfully close. I guessed she'd have her pups the following morning.

Angel was always a fine and dedicated mother whom I always trusted to take care of her pups when they arrived. She was a very special dog to me, not only because she was a beautiful malamute with a brilliant white coat and had given me many healthy pups, but because she's a strong-willed leader with a determined and fighting spirit.

That evening, fog rolled in from the Arctic Ocean, obliterating the sun's warmth, the songbirds' tunes, and the aroma of spring. The fog felt especially cold. I visited Angel before I went in the cabin for the night, but there were no pups yet. As I opened my cabin door, a strong blast of wind pulled the door from my grip. I didn't think much of it. I figured winter was over, it was late spring and a snow storm was out of the question. I fired up the oil stove, fried a fresh caribou steak for dinner and lay down on my sleeping bag. As the flame brightened in the stove I fell off to sleep.

Sometime around midnight, the cabin's windows shuttered and the stove pipe rattled, awakening me. Right away I knew it was a blizzard. Angel and her pups were my main concern. I slipped on my boots and parka and then rushed out the door. The wind almost knocked me over and the whipping snow stung my face as I worked my way toward Angel's house.

She had two newborn pups. A gray pup was suckling and the other gray and white puppy lay motionless beside Angel's hind leg. I picked up the tiny, lifeless puppy. She was wet and cold. I covered her in my hands and ran into the cabin. She was so pathetically weak and I wondered how she could ever survive. I held her in the warmth above the oil heater and messaged her chest. Her ribs felt fragile and she was not breathing. I blew lightly into her face. I massaged her again as the stove's heat warmed her. I blew again gently into her tiny mouth. She gasped and her ribs expanded.

Boss as a puppy, protecting a bone. (photo by Andrea M. Loveland)

"C'mon girl, you can do it," I whispered. Then I felt her tiny heart beat. I kept massaging her and drying her wet fur with a towel. She gasped again and then whined.

Five years later, a blizzard barreled down the valley. My lead dog led the team with a tiger's fighting spirit and determination that only arises in someone that had faced death and survived. The same frail puppy that came back to life during that horrendous springtime blizzard in the Arctic was now my lead dog. The same pup that Angel had given up for dead, that same lifeless pup that didn't stand much of a chance to survive, but somehow she did, and became a leader for my team of 22 Alaskan malamutes on our Arctic expeditions.

My wife named her Boss and that's exactly what she was.

She was the boss of the entire dog yard. Although, she weighed only about 65 lbs and was the smallest malamute I have ever had, she dominated anyone that crossed her path with such feistiness that even Nikko, a 120 lb male, succumbed to her. Her exuberant, cheerful nature mixed with that strong will was the recipe for an excellent dog, a one-in-a-million leader.

One winter, on the first day of an expedition, the weather was mild and the snow was only knee deep. I spent that day packing two freight sleds with about one ton of supplies, sorting harnesses, and attaching cables and lines. The team watched me closely. They knew the routine and they were anxious to get the expedition started.

The following day, under the gray morning light, I broke camp, placed Boss and Farmer in lead and hitched up the rest of the team. As I secured the snow hook and bear rifle atop the sled, the dogs raised their muzzles toward the clouds and gave their farewell howl. When they finished howling I gave the command to go, and the expedition was underway.

We traveled to the base of a steep hill where I made camp. It was just the first of the many hills and mountain passes that we had to climb before we got into the heart of the Brooks Range.

That night a horrible and familiar sound awakened me. It was an unmistakable, deafening sound. The blizzard blasted with hurricane force winds for a day and night and dumped a pile of snow on us.

Now, the snow was thigh deep and even with me breaking trail in front of the team on snowshoes the leaders had their work cut out for them. Usually, the heavy dogs like Farmer make the best leaders in the deep snow because they bust trail with their chest, opening a path behind my snowshoe trail for the team to follow. But beneath the fresh snow was a layer of unstable hard pack that wouldn't support Farmer and he broke through the crust and struggled with every step. The hard pack supported Boss, though. Her light weight enabled her to stay on top, and even though the fresh snow covered her neck and shoulders, she kept the team moving.

But Mother Nature wasn't done punishing us yet. Two days later, she slammed us with another blizzard and more snow, but we continued traveling with Boss leading the way and Farmer next to her helping out when he could. Every so often I placed a third lead dog beside Farmer and Boss to help break a wider trail for the team. It was a struggle for all of us. Every day we inched our way closer to the Continental Divide in the Brooks Range. Some days we averaged 1mph busting through the deepest snow and on a good day we would average 2 mph, but as long as the sleds were moving forward and the team stayed strong and healthy, I was content.

Boss continued leading the way with Farmer at her side. I added Dino, a beautiful three year old reddish white male, as the third leader beside Boss so he could learn from her how to lead. There's not a better time to start training a malamute leader than at the age of three. At this age they've almost completely matured physically and mentally and are eager to please. This desire to please is the foundation of the Alaskan malamute character, their driving force. Their world is centered on love for the musher and pleasing him or her. It's what makes these guys tick.

The team and I fought through several more blizzards, one of which lasted seven days and nights. Finally, in March, the wind and snow storms abated and when the skies cleared, I knew it was our big break. I figured we could get some open field running and make up for lost time, but that never happened. The snow got chest deep as we worked further into the mountains.

The craggy mountains looked more spectacular each day as we continued breaking trail toward them. It's hard to say when the last time a team of malamutes had traveled where we were, if ever. It may have been as long as a hundred years ago,

Dino, Boss, and Farmer in lead.

or maybe even 1,000 years have gone by since the Inuit went through the region with their Alaskan malamutes in search of game to feed their families.

March's rich blue skies and bright sun made up for all the blizzards. Every day we traveled, and Boss, Farmer, and Dino broke trail while I skied or snowshoed ahead of them. Behind me I could hear them panting, and the sled runners grinding and moaning on the cold, dry snow as we slowly worked our way higher in elevation where the mountains cast their torn and jagged shadows on us. The dogs knew they were home, where they had originated thousands of years ago. They must have felt it. Every night they raised their muzzles and sang their ancient songs toward the heavens while the Northern Lights shot overhead like a painters brush across a star speckled canvas in a spectrum of colors. The nights were crisp and cold, so cold that moisture in the atmosphere fell from the clear sky like snow. And in the mornings, I was greeted with sundogs, flaring sunrises and the sweet smell of willow smoke streaming from my tent's chimney. I was reminded of the reason I was drawn to the Arctic in the first place. Although the arctic environment can be brutally unforgiving and had nearly done me in a few times, it was all worth it.

As the team and I gained altitude, climbing higher amongst the gray limestone mountain peaks, many dall sheep nervously watched us pass by and when spring's long days captured the night skies, and snow melt dripped off the dark rocks alongside the riverbank, my sleds became light and almost empty of supplies. So, a few miles short of my goal, I stopped, swung the team around in the opposite direction and gave them the command to go. I couldn't take the gamble of completely running out of supplies just to reach my destination.

***

I'm coming up on another expedition season in the Arctic. Everything is all set—gear and dog food is piled on the trailer and the team is muscled up and rearing to go, As long as there are Alaskan malamutes like Boss, and a goal within reach for next winter, and the winter after that, and the next—the team and I will continue breaking trail.

Twenty-two malamute team taking a break on a mountain pass.

Nikko, a wheel dog, relaxing on the sled.

Wheel dogs resting after breaking trail all day.

The team taking a break on the Arctic coast.

Dino, one of my best leaders.

Our camp near the Continental Divide.

Twenty-two malamutes waiting for dinner.

Heading home after 99 days on the trail.

The team waiting for the command to go.   (photo by Germán A. Obando)

Twenty-two malamutes pulling 3 months worth of supplies.

The dog team taking a breather.

The team waiting as I snowshoe ahead of them.

The team near the Continental Divide.

Walking with the team on the Beaufort Sea. (photo by Angus Mill)

Running ahead of the team on snowshoes on the Beaufort Sea. (photo by Andrea M. Loveland)

Anticipating the command to go.

A quick nap on the sea ice.

My two biggest fans, Melvin and Elaina.